BLESSED
WITH LESS

BLESSED WITH LESS

Joel B. Parker
aka
The ≠ Poet Joel

Parker's Poetry Plus Inc. Publishing First Edition 2017
Copyright © 2017 by Joel B. Parker
Published in the USA by:
Parker's Poetry Plus Inc., Brooklyn, NY
Graphic Design by: Dexter Koonce
Research by: Kisha Cease
ISBN-13: 978-0692057421
ISBN-10: 0692057420
Printed in the United States of America
www.ParkersPoetryPlus.com

Mustard Seeds

Mustard Plant Leaf

Mustard Tree

This 2nd Book is Dedicated To:

The Youngest child of each of my biological Siblings:

(aka My Nephews and Nieces)

Yanique D. Fletcher-Jordet,

Jamila Deanda,

Mordecai J. Parker,

Able E. Parker

Approbation

Deacon Joel Parker has masterfully and unmistakably unraveled one of the best kept mysteries of the Kingdom with his book, Blessed With Less. As countless Believers sit forehead-in-hand, knees bent and lips prepared, again, to ask God for more, once again the power detailed in this work eludes them.

Does God really need to add? Does he really need to increase? Does he really need to enlarge? Although, in answer to our prayers he certainly does those things, but need to? I think not. Once we discover the message in this work we will be content to know that the same God who spoke an entire world into existence with absolutely nothing but his voice can do exceeding, abundantly more than we can ask or think ... with a measure of mustard seed faith.

He can absolutely satisfy our needs without the grandeur that so many of us crave; without the truckloads of miracles we pray for and without the super-sized phenomenon we have come to call the blessing.

I believe that God is pleased with this great work of Deacon Joel Parker, and even more pleased with the soft fragrance of simplicity and innocence woven between each line.

I can now say that I am grateful to God that I am, indeed, Blessed With Less!

Dr. Cynthia McInnis,
Associate Pastor, Executive Administrator
Full Effect Ministries

Foreword

Deacon Joel Parker is a gifted writer who has given us the book of poems "Poetically Correct, From Ground To Glory", that inspired and lifted us. He is on the list of poets that are registered in our nation's capital and considered genius in their work.

But in this writing "Blessed With Less" he gives us a prose that takes us from rhythm and rhyme and leads those of us that have an ear to hear, into a Spiritual concept and understanding about ourselves.

The world system teaches that to be "blessed" is to have more, but Joel Parker informs us of the trust we should have in a far superior system, the faith in our creator. If God holds the entire universe intact through the power of His Word, He certainly can speak over our lives and supply all of our need, according to His riches in glory, by Christ Jesus.

His book shows us; to despise not the day of small beginnings, but to realize that through faith, little (that mustard seed) becomes much, when placed in the masters hand.

I believe that "Blessed With Less" will empower, enrich, and enlighten everyone that gets their hands on it. **IT'S A MUST READ!!**

Bishop Darrell K. Dove Sr.
M.S.F.A. Vice Presider

Preface

Let me start by first re-affirming this is not an autobiographical book, however there are extremely strong personal references in as much as I am speaking from a personal perspective based on what I've experienced, studied and or personally witnessed.

Chronologically this is not the second book written, however it is the second book published. This work was imparted to me after I asked a somewhat rhetorical question. While being invited to speak before an affluent, progressive audience, many with grand political and social positions; I asked what I could possibly say to this group of people. God answered me and said, "tell them you're blessed with less". I immediately did what I would normally do, I began to write, but not in my usual poetic format. Initially I was just jotting down notes to research, then, relative concepts, ultimately it evolved into this book that you are now reading. It blessed me along the way, I pray it does the same for you.

My main objective and goal is to change the average perspective on what it means to be Blessed. Quantify the different types of blessings. Qualify what blessed isn't, and then illuminate how you are not insignificant and you can be blessed, even with less.

The ≠ Poet Joel

Acknowledgements:

My M.S.F.A. Presider Bishop Dwight P. Dove who through years of struggle, showed us how to be blessed even with less. My M.S.H.C. Pastor Bishop Darrell K. Dove Sr. who affirmed that of my many talents, this gift of writing should be pursued and used to God's glory. Coach Vaughn Edmeade who sparked the fire in this book. Patricia Lett, who encouraged and motivated me to exercise my gift to greatness. Laura Candido, who continued to tell me I had more than enough to do what I needed to do. My oldest sister Cheryl Parker, who inherently contrasted my status by assuming the role of matriarch. My other siblings the late Vincent Parker; Michael Parker, Jerry Parker, Tina Deanda and Renee Parker, who all were examples and allowed me to learn from both their achievements and their mistakes. My children and steadfast supporters, Juanita Fulmore-Wallace & Joseph Parker. All the Pastors who are in covenant fellowship with Morning Star for your preaching, consistent prayers and words of admonishment; reminding us all, what it means, and what it takes to truly be Blessed. Four individuals who supported in their own various ways but wanted no public recognition; I will affectionately refer to them as: "Stress", "Special K", "Punkette" and "CC"
I Love you all to life.

Table of Contents:

Chapter # : **Chapter Name**   Pg.#

Table of Contents:

Chapter   #   : Chapter Name   Pg.#

Preambulatory Chapter Referenced Haikus

Haiku 001 _ Luck, Chance, Superstition

You say you believe
Luck chance and superstition
All have you deceived

Haiku 002 _ Faith, Works, Consistency

Faith, what we can't see
Proof manifested through Words
and Consistency

Haiku 003 _ Pride, Doubt, Frustration

destruction for all
pride with a haughty spirit
followed by a fall

Haiku 004 _ Praise, Practice, Contentment

Praise an outward act
Practicing with Contentment
A Spirit filled fact

Haiku 005 _ Fear, Facts, Feelings

These Words all must hear
Love, Power and a sound mind
God gave us, not fear

Haiku 006 _ Power, Authority, Dominion

Power, Dominion
gives you true Authority
Despite opinion

Haiku 007 _ Less, Lack, Mediocrity

You perception views
Less, Lack, Mediocrity
Truth shows, how to see

Haiku 008 _ Position, Timing, Qualification

In place and on time
A good starting frame of mind
It can be sublime

Haiku 009 _ Greedy, Selfish, Spiteful

Ways not to succeed
Greedy, Selfish, Spiteful
Neglect others needs

Haiku 010 _ Love, Integrity, Righteousness

Valued importance
Integrity, Righteousness
Love is all of this

Haiku 011 _ Cursed, Envious, Poisoned

These can be reversed
Cursed, Envious and Poisoned
Or it can get worse

Haiku 012 _ Blessed, Ordained, Perfection

Jesus Christ gave us
A Blessed Godly connection
Ordained Perfection

Warning:

This Book is subject to Bless your life !

Chapter 1

Luck,
Chance,
Superstition

"Oh what a beautiful morning,
oh what a beautiful day"
"I have a wonderful feeling,
everything's going my way"…

This song was Composed by Richard Rodgers and Lyrics by Oscar Hammerstein II first released in 1943 in a stage play called "Oklahoma". However, in 1955 the western cowboy show was made into a movie. That song "Oh what a beautiful morning" was re-recorded many times by many great singers; most memorably by Frank Sinatra and Ray Charles individually. That song was played regularly in my hearing as a child; even without the movie, we listened to that song. Despite its slow country pace, it was still very much encouraging, causing me to feel good; but more notably, I felt extremely lucky. What other logically explainable rationale could an individual have? No matter the age, what answer could one give to qualify how everything, not just one thing or even some things, but "every thing's" going their way?

I began to pattern my life on these concepts and philosophies. I like most of my young impressionable

Chapter 1 Luck, Chance, Superstition

friends subscribed to a common belief system which we early in lives learned was passed down unwittily from every preceding generation to us. The ideology of "luck, chance and superstition" was often mistakenly referred to as blessed. As a direct result, everything we planned or did was based on this previously mentioned mindset; even our diet was affected. Considering this, we would start the day with what many would consider to be the most important meal of the day. My favorite cold breakfast cereal was "Lucky Charms". Although high in nutritional value ratings, and enriched with Vitamin D; what caught my immediate attention was the name: Lucky Charms. Not to mention the box cover showing graphically eye-catching pictures of toasted circler oats, multi-colored marshmallows in various very familiar shapes, in an abundance. One little known trivia type fact is that "Lucky Charms" was the 1st breakfast cereal to include marshmallow pieces. These marshmallows were in the shapes of green four-leaf clovers, pink hearts, orange shooting stars, pots of gold, red balloons, purple horseshoes, rainbows, yellow moons, green trees, blue diamonds, and the mascot was a Leprechaun. The catch-phrase slogan was: "They're Magically Delicious". We'd pour bowls upon bowls picking through that cereal looking for our favorite charm.

We weren't allowed to waste food and were constantly reminded that there were many "less fortunate" individuals starving. Therefore, we ate every single bit of the content in that cereal box, but there was still an exciting sense of fulfilment finding our specific individual favorite charm. In October 2012, Lucky charms reported sales exceeding, two hundred fifty million dollars for just that calendar year making them the seventh (7th) largest cold cereal brand; note an amazing 46% of adults to this day consume this product. Do you think it's because of the nutritional value, the taste or an imbedded belief in luck?

Near my residence there was a walk-in "OTB" Off Track Betting store. In this establishment, you could legally bet on race horses without physically going to the track; hence the name "off Track". These gamblers felt they were "Lucky" that they didn't have to be subjected to the smell of the horses which they were betting on. They were willing to take a chance on a horse they had never seen or sometimes never even heard of. Sometimes it was the name, the number, the color the jockey was wearing, or just the odds. Although multiple locations were in existence, all over the country, patrons would boast how their location had the best luck. In 2008 the OTB Corporation filed for chapter nine (9) bankruptcy, announcing to the world, they were more than five (5) hundred million dollars in the red and in 2010 they closed nearly fifty (50) locations. Even though "OTB" generated billions of dollars, most would in deference to the concept simply say, they're luck ran out.

Many people say they are lucky, they have an object which they consider to be a lucky charm. The charm could have been constructed from almost anything; I have seen charms made of leather, wood, skin, bone, metal and plastic. When an individual says that they are feeling lucky, they at that moment are more inclined to engage in some activity containing risks. From gambling to soliciting company from a companion or even a stranger. No matter what the stakes or odds against them might be or have been, the feeling of luck deluded them into taking a chance. There are only estimates from that time of how many illegal gambling clubs, bookies or number runners existed but I'm sure most would agree there were more illegal than legal ones. In this current time, you can find some form of "legal" gambling almost everywhere including gas stations and your local corner grocery store. One of the most popular slogans advertised on television and in newspapers across the country is "a dollar and a dream".

In the Charlie Brown Peanuts saga Linus had a lucky blanket, and many regardless of their race, creed, color, ethnicity and even religion claim to have the "luck of the Irish". Can you remember your favorite "lucky" object, item or garment that you attributed to you having a more positive outcome? Winning a bet or competition, getting a date, landing a job or a promotion? Was it a horseshoe, wishbone, rabbit's foot, four-leaf clover, or perhaps a lucky kiss?

In my late teens I had what I liked to call my "lucky go get a job suit". When I wore that Blue and Grey Herringbone suit I sincerely believed I would obtain what-ever job I applied to and or interviewed for. Why this was even a consideration or a thought some would ask. Does anybody remember the Nike commercial where the slogan was "it's gotta be the shoes"? Well I thought it just had to be the suit; as a matter of fact, when wearing that suit, I had an absolute 100% (one hundred percent) interview/hired success rate. I believed in it so much that I gifted that very same suit to an individual who was convinced he didn't have any luck and couldn't get a job. He had limited education, limited to no job experience and a minor criminal record. All realistic obstacles, however, he obtained not one (1) but two (2) jobs with-in 3(three) hours of putting on my suit; including travel time. Are there some relative factors, yes, but did my suit really get any of those jobs? Did that suit make either one of us more job worthy, or did we just have on a very nice suit that we both wore well? In the political arena, the color suit and or tie are subject to the particular political party and the occasion thereof. That's not luck that is preference and protocol.

On the other hand, there is another variation of luck that is not so popular; that's knock-on wood; "bad luck". Based on the same principals it is the negative aspect of uncontrollable circumstances. Athletes have attributed many failed games to a missing lucky something or other. Sometimes it was a piece of jewelry, or a garment; "my lucky socks". Even if that garment was laundered, for some they would say that you washed the luck off. Many still rely on their lucky mascot. Others had to perform a ritual in a very specific manner; a certain amount of brush strokes on their hair, rubbing a belly in a certain direction, a chant or a motivational affirmation.

Many people smoked Tabaco products, however one of the top selling brands of cigarettes I recall people saying effected their outcome was the brand called "Lucky Strikes". Most of the people who smoked them weren't addicted, but felt it gave them a certain look or status which they believed affected their environment. The same hold true with types of alcoholic beverages. Think about it, you can propose a toast with almost anything in your glass. However, the drink of choice to "wish luck" is qualified by the importance of the event and quantified by the cost or value of the beverage.

Merriam Webster dictionary defines Luck as: 1. something that happens to a person by or as if by chance. 2. the accidental way things happen". There are over fifty (50) globally recognized symbols of luck. Not including the personal ones, we make up ourselves on our own for our own occasions. It's amazing how many people subscribe to luck, chance, and superstitions. Most also strongly believe that there is absolutely nothing that can be done to remedy the way the cards of life are dealt. While that may be true, I prefer to hold to the old saying "you can see my hand, but you can't play it". In short that simply means you may not be able to control what is dealt to you in life, but you do have a say on how you handle what is dealt to you. However, the norm says go about your day most times unconsciously performing generations of ordinances, rituals and routines in a certain sequence hoping for a happily ever after ending.

We rush trying to quickly close an umbrella while in doors; because one belief is that an open umbrella in doors will prevent marriage. If our left palm itches, we will receive money but won't be able to keep it. If you wore shoes to a grave site, you must not wear them into the house, or you'll carry death in the house with you. Even though common sense tells us that it exists many buildings don't display the thirteenth floor. The elevator just goes direct from twelve to fourteen. We Knock on wood and or throw salt over our shoulder, to reverse bad luck. Panic if a black cat crosses our path, take several steps backward in order to be on the same side of a pole or tree noting that it's bad luck to "split the pole". Some even fold their money in a certain way denoting one direction causes you to lose it and the other to retain it. According to millions, a broken mirror equals seven years of bad luck. "Step on a crack, break your back". This list seemingly doesn't end. Simply consider the basis of most horror movies.

Note I am in no way shape or form glorifying or promoting any of these practices; however, I do believe the enemy is easier to defeat if you understand that it is indeed an enemy. It has been said that abolitionist Harriet Tubman made this statement "I freed a thousand slaves; I could have freed more if only they knew they were slaves". More times than not our biggest obstacle and opposition is not an outside enemy but our own "inner me". Most don't consciously recognize this as a tactic of the true enemy. Most consider luck as simply chance; a mere coincidence or an uncontrollable happenstance. Also referred to as fate, fortune, karma, the stars, kismet and or serendipitous. Then there are those who subscribe to actual rituals including but not limited to superstitions and even incantations.

One of the most interesting rituals to me, was performed by former NFL Player John (*Big John*) Henderson. This man played professional football from 2002-2011. He stood 6' 7" tall and weighed over 350lbs. His pregame ritual was to have his training coach or substitute slap him in the face as hard as they could. Noting that was his motivation and he believed it would give him a better game. He is not the only one with an unusual ritual. LSU Tigers (Louisiana State University) Football coach Les Miles would eat grass from the playing field during pregame activities. Miles said his pre-game ritual "humbles (him) as a man" and that "it lets (him) know that (he's) part of the field and part of the game." I wouldn't want you to think this was just a practice in football.

Major league baseball player Steven James Kline played professionally from 1997-2007. He ritualistically would wear the same dirty hat all season without ever washing it, stating "the dirt kept him grounded and reminded him where he came from. You also will not find peanuts in a shell being sold at a NASCAR event because they consider the shells bad luck. Hall of Famer Glen "Mr. Goalie" Hall holds the NHL record for consecutive games started. Hall has said that at some point, it didn't feel like he was "giving everything (he) had" unless he before each game made himself regurgitate. Even the great NBA legend Michael Jordan wore his North Carolina College shorts under his NBA uniform shorts throughout his entire career. In contrast, Professional Tennis Player Andre Agassi doesn't wear underwear during games and believes that helps him to win. There are hundreds of examples, but each one somehow made those individuals feel either lucky or unlucky.

In the 1971 movie "Dirty Harry" Clint Eastwood while during a standoff with a man who had just robbed a bank asked a question most with any age on them are familiar with. There he stood holding in his hand a 44 magnum, the bank robber on the ground reaching for his shotgun. Eastwood asked the robber "do you feel lucky"? Eastwood repeated himself while demeaning the man by calling him a punk. How lucky would you feel if someone was pointing one of the most powerful handguns in the world at you? Now add these additional factors: you're black, the person holding that gun is a white law enforcement officer, you are on the ground bleeding from a gunshot wound you received during the bank robbery which led you to this point, time and position. The inquisitive criminal conceded with a nonverbal gesture and defeat in his posture. But he wanted to know if he made the right choice, so he asked, only to find out he hadn't. The shotgun he was reaching for was loaded but Eastwood's 44 was empty.

Therefore, I conclude that even though he was a criminal element, he could have taken the chance, and most probably changed his situation. Only if he had made a more calculated assessment and not relied on luck. If the outcome of the situation could be manipulated by your action(s) is it still in deed luck? How much more of an opportunity for changing outcomes are there for those who subscribe to a belief system. For those who acknowledge there must be a higher power and for those who have an inkling but can't identify it, they use clichés. Thomas Jefferson once said, "I'm a greater believer in luck, and I find the harder I work the more I have of it". This leads me to ask from an educated logical perspective, why anyone would rely on luck when the very basis of it alludes to the notion that there is no God. Luck is a belief in everything which amounts to believing in nothing, it's like having several true loves. Luck says that there is nothing that is absolute and no one entity is in control. Yet many still equate success with luck and ask, have you had any luck with your job search, the test you took, or your loan application? People of God should not subscribe to and or rely on luck but on the Alpha and Omega, the all wise God. When asked about God, "Scientists have calculated that the chances of something so patently absurd actually existing are millions to one. However, according to the English author: Sir Terrence David John "Terry" Pratchett, mere "magicians have calculated that million-to-one chances crop up nine times out of ten". Ironically drastically increasing the probability rate to 90%. In Las Vegas Nevada, the gambling capital of the world, people come from miles away to take a chance. As any who has seriously gambled knows, "the house" always wins. In fact, if you win too much, that is too frequent and or too large of a quantity, you're subject to observation, detention, interrogation, and possibly physical bodily harm. This is so because the powers that be, believe and most certainly know, you cheated. The irony; even gambling institutions have a belief system that is not attributed to luck or chance; they clearly don't believe that anyone could be that lucky.

If it's not luck or chance, then maybe it's superstition, which Webster defines as: a belief or way of behaving that is based on fear of the unknown and faith in magic or luck. A notion maintained despite evidence to the contrary. Do you believe in magic, or do you like most who believe performances are just illusions and the rest the power of suggestion? The full definition of superstition states that it is a belief or practice resulting from ignorance, fear of the unknown, trust in magic or chance, or a false conception of causation. One concept some many dispute, as to whether it be false or truth; astrology. Many would say that it is not part of any superstition but scientifically documented facts. However, the definition of astrology states that it is: the study of movements of celestial bodies interpreted as having an influence on human affairs and the natural world. This alludes to the notion that there is some other entity at the very least affecting, if not totally controlling us humans and this world. Note the Bible is full of references denoting celestial and terrestrial beings. If that is not superstition, then it must be belief in a higher power, because an equal power wouldn't be able to "control" elements and us, so intelligent beings. Fact, there is some relevance to the astrological alignment and seasons. These signs do have a general form of order. However, since they are seasonal, I treat them like the weather or a thermometer. Noting it had snowed when the calendar stated that it was summer. It has been hot in the season of winter. You can further note that thermometers and barometers only gauge what the temperature and other variations of the climate are. However, a thermostat dictates and controls what that temperature will be. If the weather was regulated by luck chance or superstitions, it would be equally unstable and totally unpredictable. There would be no logical trace of causation.

In conclusion, I contend, although relative, Astrology, astronomy, and cosmology are studies involving theories that are relevant and relative but not absolute. There are people born the same day and year as me, but we are completely opposite. Let me be clear, there is a difference

Chapter 1 Luck, Chance, Superstition

in believing something exists and subscribing to or believing in it. I believe the Nazi commander Adolph Hitler existed, I further believe he had great leadership abilities, but I have no faith confidence or belief in him. I believe witchcraft exists, but is that belief the basis on which things exist? On the contrary, everything is controlled and determined by God. I refuse to allow anything that can be manipulated to govern my character, actions and or my very life. Doris day sang a song "Que Sera Sera" meaning what will be, will be; I say no, not necessarily. For the power of life and death lies in the tongue, but that only applies to those who subscribe to, believe in and practice the word of God. All others are subject to the ideology and works of this physical natural astrological order. Those works are carried out by their perception and philosophies.

Do you still feel lucky? As you get older do you take the same chances you did as a child? When your luck runs out where is your hope? Do you subscribe to the very superstitious writing on the wall? After assessing the facts of this matter, I've come to the conclusion that all along we were subscribing to luck, chance and or superstition and unwittingly calling it blessed. I now fully understand, and rest assured that we should not subscribe to the unstable, unpredictable thought of luck, chance or superstition. That will increase and most certainly assure our potential to be blessed. Truly blessed people know that God is a calculated, concise, precise creator and planner. Everyone is entitled to their own beliefs; the final question we must all ask ourselves is what and or in what or in whom do we believe?

Chapter 2

Faith,
Works,
Consistency

Do you have faith? If so, have you ever questioned your faith? If you are like most humans, at some point in time I am sure you have. If you are not sure whether you have faith, that in and of itself is a question of faith. There may be some confusion as to what true faith is. Faith, by definition is: 1. complete trust or confidence in someone or something. 2. strong belief in God or in doctrines of a religion, based on spiritual apprehension rather than proof. However, the bible says it in the book of Hebrews chapter 11 like this: "Now Faith is the substance of things hoped for, the evidence of things not seen". At first, I had a strong contention with the dictionary definition of faith because it states that faith is something that cannot be proved. I have since resolved my distain because they made an unignorably strong and relevant point. True faith can sometimes be confused with delusion or even superstition. Many have believed things that others could not see, thus hard to prove. Several of those individuals turned out to be declared geniuses. People like Albert Einstein, Hunter S. Thompson, Vincent Van Gogh, Sigmund Freud and Aristotle; they were all able to see things on a different level; from an abstract, outside of the box view. This mindset reminds me of a poem written in 1899 by

Chapter 2 Faith, Works, Consistency

American educator and poet William Hughes Mearns,
entitled: **"Antigonish"**

Yesterday, upon the stair,

I met a man who wasn't there

He wasn't there again today

I wish, I wish he'd go away...

When I came home last night at three

The man was waiting there for me

But when I looked around the hall

I couldn't see him there at all!

Go away, go away,

don't you come back any more!

Go away, go away, and please don't slam the door...

(slam!)

Last night I saw upon the stair

A little man who wasn't there

He wasn't there again today

Oh, how I wish he'd go away...

Blessed With Less

This poem was inspired by reports of the ghost of a man roaming the stairs of a haunted house in Antigonish, Nova Scotia, Canada. The poem was originally part of a play called "the Psycho-ed" and was written for an English class at Harvard University. The faculty thought it was abstract, but so amazing.

Have you ever heard something that no one else around you admitted to hearing? Or have you seen something that no one else around admitted they saw? Did you second guess yourself, or were you absolutely sure you heard what you heard, or saw what you saw? For some this is just double talk, but those who understand the complexity of the world we live in, they also generally operate in a different realm.

I see faith as being a complex   metaphysical intangible, yet at the same time it is as basic or common as the word belief. (Meta) a Greek prefix(beyond) to the base "Physical" (nature) gives you the combined word metaphysical. Meta is defined as: (of a creative work) referring to itself or to conventions of its genre; self-referential. In art the term is used to characterize something that is. Metaphysical is defined as: 1. of or relating to metaphysics. 2a. of or relating to the transcendent or to a reality beyond what is perceptible to the senses. 2b. supernatural. 3. Highly abstract or abstruse; also: theoretical.

Intangible is defined as: unable to be touched or grasped; not having a physical presence. Difficult or impossible to define or understand; vague and abstract. The following are all clear examples of intangibles: Free, God,

Chapter 2 Faith, Works, Consistency

Goodwill, Gravity, Joy, Light, Love, Responsibility, Truth and Wind. We experience most of these things almost every day, regardless as to whether we acknowledge, recognize, and or identify with them. We experience them regardless of our race, creed, status, stature, or financial portfolio. Usually when we refer to any of these we wind up giving an example of how it is exhibited as opposed to a definitive definition or even explanation.

There are many people walking around who are not enslaved in the traditional manner that most recognize, yet they are bound. Whether it is emotionally, financially, geographically or spiritually. The concept of who and or what God is varies from country city household and individual. Goodwill is subjective. I've had prisoners tell me that if it weren't for them law enforcement would not exist, so we should be grateful for their "goodwill" toward mankind that they created and maintain a viable work environment. Gravity is serious, heaviness or weight, ambiguous and not specific. What makes one joyful, is as extreme as a sadist or masochist and their manner or mode in which they obtain their pleasure. Light can be shaded but not confined; unlike water which needs help to direct its flow, light shines independently in every direction. Some would say a mercy killing is love. The only one-word definition of love is God, which is another intangible. Responsibility is subjected to what we as individuals impose on ourselves. If someone asks us to do something we don't want to do, we quickly tell them "that's not my job or responsibility. It is said that truth is what you believe to be true. There is emotional truth, factual truth, legal truth, and technical truth; truth is a fact or belief that is accepted as true. Wind commonly referred to as air is invisible to the naked eye, and needed for us humans to breathe; but in a tornado or hurricane, completely overwhelming, even breath taking. Faith, dare I say is greater than all of these. Just because it cannot be seen with the natural eye doesn't mean we shouldn't believe in it.

You can have confidence and or faith in almost anything. Any Deity, entity and or object, be it Celestial, terrestrial, visible or invisible; in this earthly realm or in another galaxy. What is the foundation of your belief? Is it political, philosophical, physical, moral, spiritual or scientific. Ironically many hold their confidence in things they haven't even tried to understand. Usually an idea or tradition imposed on us without an explanation. Dr. Joy Leary wrote an extensive study on "Post Traumatic Slave Syndrome". In that study, it exposes how much creatures of habit we are. We repeat what we see even when it's not comfortable. We believe it because that is the way we've seen it done. It is quite common, normal and completely understandable to have a level of confidence in yourself, even when we don't understand ourselves, mostly because we don't know who we are. However, if one doesn't submit to a higher power that individual may become self-righteous. Confidence is very similar to faith however faith in general is most often used when referring to another entity.

Faith contrasts luck, chance and superstition. It allows us to have complete confidence in a deity and or entity that we can know although we are not able to fully comprehend. Don't allow your lack of understanding to sway your level of belief. Take for instance something simple like the common cold. Most everyone has had a cold, but medical science cannot produce a single absolute cure or preventive medicine for it. In fact, doctors don't really study prevention they thrive on treatment. Neither can they say definitively where it comes from, but they've narrowed it down to just over 200 (two hundred) strains of viruses which are implicated as the cause. Does that in any way shape or form change whether we believe it exists? Right now, some thorough analytical reader is saying "don't trust things you don't understand", unfortunately there are not some, but many things we, in this finite human state that will never understand. On one occasion, the Apostle Paul "stood in the midst of Mars' hill, and said, Ye men of Athens, I perceive that in all things ye are too superstitious. For as I passed by, and beheld your devotions, I found an altar with this inscription, TO THE UNKNOWN GOD" (Acts 17:22-23). But he cleared that up immediately, preaching to them Jesus. Mankind is frail but God is infinite, almighty and sovereign. He will give you an understanding of things you need, if you enter a relationship with Him.

Isn't it intriguing that almost every entity of belief is required in formal education except "religion"? Philosophy and politics are part of global history. That history is indicative of the power in place. The political perspective shown in most lessons favors the "politically correct party of that administration. When this country was formed, it's history portrayed native American Indians who were already here and functioning, as savages. Anatomy is the physical and medical part of science. For years, this country taught racial inequality, noting that one race was genetically superior to the other. Evolution is the philosophical aspect of the same science. Its premise is that the earth and all life forms therein were created by a cataclysmic explosion. Moving forward it states one race was portrayed as evolving more rapid and in a more advanced manner than the other.

As intelligent and informed as scientists are, how can one believe that an accidental explosion created planets in a perfectly aligned solar system that rotate on a precise axis continually. How can one further believe that human life also evolved from that same incident? The complexity of mankind, each individual having distinguishably different finger prints, DNA, and retina registration; highly improbable. Morality is governed by the consensus of the specified power in place of that current time. All actions were justified as morally good for those in power, but morally bad for those considered subservient. From 1619-1865 slavery in the United States was legal, therefore morally accepted. Somehow even after it was legally abolished it thrived in its same form another fifty (50) years. Now it has evolved and is exhibited in different forms, nonetheless it still exists and is still deemed moral in the eyes of the empowered oppressors. In abiding with moral law, one is taught that they must subscribe and concede to whatever the norm says even if the norm isn't normal.

Moreover, if an individual were to oppose, or even disagree with the powers that be, they are immediately considered and labeled, contrary and rebellious. The amount and level of education one is provided or even offered is contingent on their economic, social and or class status. How many other things are needed but not part of the mandatory curriculum? Nowhere does our education system require us to study the religious or spiritual side of man. After many years of misinformation, and domination, what is one to believe in, and how does one even begin? My faith is in God and comes from the words written in the Bible. "Now faith is the substance of things hoped for, the evidence of things not seen. (Hebrews 11:1). It continues in vs 6 by stating: "But without faith it is impossible to please Him; for he that cometh to God must believe that He is, and that He is a rewarder of them that diligently seek Him". In the book of Romans 10:17 the Apostle Paul writes: "Faith Cometh by hearing, and hearing by the word of God".

Faith is more than memorizing or reciting repeatedly passages of scripture. It is more than knowing the ordinances and order of service. Reading and learning it is essential, but its essence is knowing how to apply it; that is life giving. Faith is an action word, thus "faith without works is dead" (James 2:20). Truly no matter what you claim that you believe, if you do nothing to qualify what you believe it is just a good idea. In contrast works without faith is just labor and is also dead. Clearly, it is necessary to work to sustain your natural self. How much more should we work for God? What by the means of your physical works have you accomplished? What was your motive for ritualistically showing up or performing? Was it for money, power, prominence? Did you learn anything? Did you better yourself? Do you know more about God and what He requires? If you believe in God then you should believe and know, He has a purpose and a plan specifically for you. If one is going to work, one should strive to understand what it is they believe in. When I say, I believe in God, a very genuine question arises. Who and what is God? What or who do I believe Him to be?

"The Lord our God is one Lord" Deuteronomy 6:4. Although you might not be able to recognize Him for all that He is. He has manifested Himself in so many ways that many were confused into believing that there were many gods. There was a god for every element you could imagine. Including the sun god, moon god a fire god and even a sex god. You may know Him as a doctor, lawyer, healer, way maker, provider, deliverer or even savior. He is King of Kings, Lord of Lords, Alpha and Omega, the beginning and the end. In short, He's everything to me and everything we need. God is a spirit and they that worship Him must do so in spirit and in truth. God the spirit speaks to the spirit man for the fleshly carnal mind is enmity or an enemy to God (Romans 8:7).

God gets no glory in flesh (John 6:63). God in His infinite wisdom has given every single human the measure of faith (Hebrews 12:3). That is the inert ability to believe and know there is a higher power; but it is left to us to choose whether we subscribe and yield to that power. Although true worship is a state of mind, it must be followed by actions. If left to simply belief in God's existence, then we are doomed and no better than the devil who also believes and trembles. (James 2:19). The work you do even if you say it's in the name of the Lord is not what constitutes true belief. But that work is an extension and outward display of how you are supposed to feel about God and will be tried by the very God you claim that you are working for. Many in that day, yes the final judgement day, will claim the work they did was for Him (Matthew 7:21-23). How do you think He will respond to you? Will He know who you are in a positive intimate manner ?

Have you ever asked yourself who you are truly working for? Is it for fame, fortune, accolades, power or for God? Was the work you did a one-time event? Are you a part time believer? Although most believe in the "ten commandments" and basic biblical principles. Are you one of the many people who come to the house of worship for weddings funerals and the major occasions? Ironically, the same cycle is almost paralleled in the following three major religions:

In **Judaism**, they attend the Temple or Synagogue:

1. Rosh Hashanah (New Year),
2. Yom Kippur, (Atonement)Holiest
3. Sukkot(Commemorates Wilderness)

In **Islam**, they go to the Mosque, Masjid, Sajada:

1. Ramadan, (revealing of the Koran),
2. Eid-al-Adha(Sacrifice Feast)Holiest
3. Hijra(New Year).
   There five pillars are: Faith, Prayer,
   Donation, Fasting and Pilgrimage.

In **Christianity**, we go to church, house of the Lord:

1. Easter(Resurrection)
2. Mother's Day (Non-Religious, but a
   day we honor our Mothers)
3. New Year's (Pray the old year out
   and for a healthy, prosperous New Year).

Blessed With Less

Are you one who comes all the time but you're inactive, because you believe it's someone else's job to function as the church? With that mentality, how many of those appearances do you think God is accepting and or honoring? imagine going to school, having perfect attendance but no class participation, no homework no test scores and add bad behavior; what grade would you reasonably expect? Faith should govern your life every day. Daily one must ask if the actions displayed in public or private reflect what you believe. Do my actions prove who or what I am? James, the brother of Jesus said, "shew me thy faith without thy works and I'll shew thee my faith by my works" (James 2:18). Much more so than your natural job where you cannot consistently miss work, with or without a reasonable excuse, have poor work ethic when you are there and then show up expecting a lucrative paycheck.

God is looking for people with unwavering faith in Him. The Hebrew boys, Shadrach, Meshach and Abednego believed God so much, so they said they were not going to bow to the pagan king despite the fiery furnace which they were threatened with. Their faith said God is able, He will deliver. But if not, yes even if He chose not to deliver them, they were going to obey Him and not bow to idols.

Faith is more than just a religion it is the motivating factor to a life style. That life style should be in alignment with what Gods Word says and in consistent behavior. For those who say they don't believe in religion. Religion is just a practice. So, if you religiously or ritualistically bathe, brush your teeth, eat or sleep, that not necessarily a bad practice. When people see you daily they shouldn't have to wonder if you are living a Godly life. Jesus said He would be in us "a well of living water springing up into everlasting life" (John 4:14). Living water is not still or stagnant but continually moving and that is how believers should be. Just as running water purifies itself, it is the constant movement that strengthens us. "Therefore, my beloved brethren, be ye stedfast, unmoveable, always abounding in the work of the Lord, forasmuch as ye know your labour is not in vain in the Lord" (1st Corinthians 15:58). That unmoveable doesn't mean literally don't physically move. Just as Exodus 14:13 where "Moses said unto the people, Fear ye not, stand still and see the salvation of the Lord, which He will show you to day". These scriptural terms come from the same mindset which instructs us to literally keep moving, but not in our might. Rather settle ourselves in the strength of God. For it is God's battle but we still must physical show up. But it is our faith that we have to put into action. For all things are possible to him that believeth (Mark 10:27). If your faith is put into action, exhibited through your consistent work, you are now positioning yourself to be blessed.

Chapter 3

Pride,
Doubt,
Frustration

Pride (Latin, superbia) is considered to be, one of the worse of the seven deadly sins. Although not labeled "the seven" in the Bible they are all specifically called by their individual name and there are seven of them. Considering in retrospect the six others: lust (Latin, luxuria), gluttony (Latin, gula), greed / avarice: (Latin, avarita), sloth (Latin, acedia), wrath (Latin, ira) and envy (Latin, Invidia). Not to be confused with having pride in your personal achievements, or self-esteem. On the contrary, this pride is an inordinate self-esteem, commonly known as conceit. The ambiguity of the English language can sometimes be confusing. Parents teach us as children to have some pride in ourselves. The pride parents speak about is, self-confidence. The motivation to carry out your daily tasks. The drive to present work with a spirit of excellence and the satisfactory sense of accomplishment.

When you are told to go and make your parents proud, there is no negative connotation. There is no sign of deliberate disrespect, nor inference of grandeur. Only a spirit willing to please. The reasonable self-respecting aspect of pride is acceptable and very different from the delusional or arrogantly contemptable pride that God

Chapter 3 Pride, Doubt, Frustration

detests. In the very beginning of mankind, referenced in Genesis the fourth chapter. Two brothers Cain and Abel both bought and presented offerings before the Lord. God respected and was pleased with the younger brother, Abel's Animal offering. However, He wasn't pleased with the offering which Cain bought from the ground. God didn't accept it, Cain immediately got angry; God replied by telling Cain if he did well his would also be accepted. Clearly the substance that was presented, was not the problem but rather the presenter. The attitude and manner with which they were presented was unacceptable. Abel presented the first and the best, Cain on the other hand without sincere thought threw something together. Instead of Cain accepting his shortcoming, repenting and bringing an acceptable gift, he killed his brother. This pride evolved into an arrogance, jealously and hatred. When our frustrations are allowed to fester, the outcome can be devastating. Such as it was with this case, which led to murder. Killing your contemporary or what you may deem as "the competition" doesn't then make your actions acceptable. Whether it is literally physical, mental, emotional, spiritual or political murder, you are still a killer, and all sin is unacceptable.

I metaphorically likened Cain to a seven-watt light bulb, and Abel to a hundred-watt light bulb. Abel was shining bright before God. Cain putting out Abel's light didn't make Cain shine any brighter, he is still only a seven-watt bulb. Although he is the only light visible, his light was not sufficient for God. In fact, his dimness illuminated how unsatisfactory the presentation of his gift was. There are people who surround themselves with others who have the ability or lack thereof to make them look good. Pointedly some keep subordinates who are smart and skilled near them knowing they can take the credit. Others keep dysfunctional people around to help make them look competent. Frustration tends to cloud out thought process. Pride causes us to act on our emotions as opposed to what we know. What we know often gets confusing because we allow doubt to guide our minds. Unfortunately, Cain clearly didn't think this through. Not only did he kill his only brother, but now there was no other peers to contend with or be compared to. He inherited a higher level of responsibility and accountability, having to now do his job and the job of his dead brother. No one left to blame when things go wrong. Cain wanted the same respect from God, that God had for his brother, even though he didn't deserve it. That is some kind of pride.

"Pride goeth before destruction and an haughty spirit before a great fall" (Proverbs 16:18). Why so harsh some might ask. Pride is the ultimate sin of Lucifer. (Isaiah 14:12-14). Pride in short is when you strongly desire to be more than, and subsequently attempt to take Glory which belongs to God. Somewhere preceding his fall, you have to concede that he at some point began to doubt God. Even to the point of believing he could be equal or above God. He was frustrated not being number one. He then acted on his emotions, forgetting or being delusional enough to allow his pride to rebel against the almighty God. "All manner of sin and blasphemy shall be forgiven unto men: but blasphemy against the Holy Ghost shall not be forgiven unto men" (Matthew 12:31). For those misguided souls who have heard God is a loving God and will forgive us for everything, herein lies one of the exceptions. What is blasphemy and what does it have to do with pride? Blasphemy is defined as: the act or offence of speaking sacrilegiously about God or sacred things. However, blasphemy biblically is worse than the dictionary definition. One of the reasons the dictionary cannot grasp the depth and true essence is because it is a spiritual offence. Our human legalistic rationally logical mind, just cannot comprehend spiritual things. This is more than an insult or lack of reverence it is utter contempt. In order for one to blaspheme against the Holy Ghost, one must have it indwelling. People without the Holy Ghost are speaking and acting out of ignorance or misinformation. Those are the type of people that Jesus instructed us to continually pray for. On the cross, He himself said "Father forgive the for they know not what they do" Luke 23:34.

In contrast 1st John 5:16 says "There is a sin unto death: I do not say that he shall pray for it". This level of blasphemy is not an error or mistake. It is in fact a deliberate conscious informed decision that says you know God from a personal experience, but you choose not to submit. Moreover, you now denounce God and refuse to reverence His divine eminence. An individual with this much distain for an entity that once dwelled and empowered them is utterly unfathomable. This pride filled person is so full of them self that they leave no room to be redeemed, mainly because they view themselves as equal, better and or greater than the redeemer. What can you offer someone who truly believes they have more than you? Moreover, what will they accept from you? They will ultimately act unconscionably, in as much as they see no one as able, or good enough to correct them. There is no acceptable consequence for their behavior. When dealing with this type of heady individual, you will find often, that they have a superiority complex. Hence you can sin against man and that's bad enough, but it becomes worse when that person you sin against is a servant of God; or God Himself.

For those who will argue that Abel was not really a servant but possibly merely a child; the Gospel of Matthew 18:6 States "whoso shall offend one of the least of these little ones that believe in me, it is better for him that a millstone were hanged about his neck, and he were drowned in the depth of the sea". 1st Chronicles states, "touch not mine anointed, and do my prophets no harm". For those who will argue that Abel wasn't a prophet, that same book of Matthew 25:40 continues saying "But Inasmuch as ye have done it unto one of the least of the of these my brethren, ye have done it unto me". Pride is the absence of humility. Proverbs 6:16-19 expounds on some things that God hates. On the top of that list is a "proud Look". Pride has a distinguishable posture and character; a personal attribute or attitude taken on, based on that persons' lack of belief in anything other than them self. This brings us to the root of where that lack forms.

Doubt is a feeling of uncertainty, or lack of conviction; the complete opposite of faith. "So then faith cometh by hearing" (Romans 10:17), a familiar passage of scripture. But have you considered that doubt also comes from hearing. The difference is the later part of that same passage in Romans says, "and hearing by the word of God", however doubt is usually a diluted or misinterpreted

Chapter 3 Pride, Doubt, Frustration

version of those same words. Or worse an intentional perverted word sewn in your hearing. It is easy to doubt almost anything or anyone. Hence any time you hear and receive a lie you increase your doubt. Human nature unction's us to believe and receive negative or derogatory information, even when we haven't vetted the source. People in general like gossip. However, some things heard are difficult to believe, most often if it involves someone we like. Doubt is a feeling, an emotionally driven perspective. Depending on what you hear, when you hear it and how you hear it could drastically shape your view. Intentional mass misinformation has been used throughout history. However, the terms "brainwashing and mind control techniques" came into common language the 1950's while discussing the treatment of soldiers in prison camps during the Korean war. There propaganda was spread affecting many. Some merely began to question the motives and methodology of the United states, and doubted some to the extreme of defecting. Doubt breeds helplessness, and helplessness breeds hopelessness. In (1st Corinthians 15:19, the Apostle Paul said, "if in this life only we have hope in Christ, we are of all men most miserable". Consider the plethora of things throughout your life that you dismissed solely because it just didn't seem probable. We continually quote a scripture, sometimes in jest; "all things are possible", but do we really believe it? Even when it is possible, based on our general outlook of life we still doubt it's probability. The sun is shining bright, but the meteorologist predicts rain. Or there is an overcast and the prediction is there will be no rain, do we believe what we see or what we hear? In the book of Ecclesiastes, the 3rd chapter, the wise man Solomon States "To everything there is a season, and a time to every purpose under heaven." It continues through eight verses listing contrasts of life. Time to be born, and a time to die; planting vs harvesting; Killing vs healing; weeping vs laughing; mourning vs dancing; getting vs losing; rending vs sewing; speaking vs silence; love vs hate; and war vs peace. However, there is no record there or in any other scripture that gives an occasion to doubt.

Most non-believers have a lack of confidence in God's word, they just cannot grasp the foundational concept. Unable to theologically explain, this is how they would describe and present the immaculate conception and plan of salvation: they would first challenge the validity of a virgin, because the only ones they believe are virgins are only so because of their age. But for argument sake this is how I've heard them tell the story; (so a virgin, without having any physical intimate relations with a man became impregnated. This occurred while she was engaged to another man. His true biological father is invisible and he through a spirit impregnated her with a physical incarnation of himself). The man she's engaged to stays with her even though he knows he's never touched her therefore making it impossible for him to be the father. And this child grows and is now a homeless man who riding into town on a donkey is announced as a King and the savoir. But he must first be abused, rejected and ultimately die. But not to worry, He will be raised from the grave and sin will then be defeated. And we the people will now be free from the sting of death. They say this with contempt, doubt and complete unbelief. Doubt becomes unbelief and in one city, even Jesus limited His "mighty works" all due to the unbelief of the people. Know for a surety, He could have performed miracles, but His plan and way is by faith by choice.

How can anyone have an intimate experience with God and then wonder, or down? Some raised with strict teaching would shudder at the thought of questioning God. Note, I can understand seeking clarity, thus questioning with an earnest, sincere desire to know and understand what's happened or is happening. Most we'll say they aren't questioning or arguing with God. Most will claim they are questioning and or qualifying the people who claim to be messengers of God. it is human nature to be curious, and the super cyber information highway encourages questioning everything. Community advocates, news reporters, and organizations with sites like "Wiki Leaks" promote investigating and challenging all reports and their sources. However, that line of questioning and the posture you take, especially with respect to God and or His representatives, needs to be respectful. But to be brazen enough to question the integrity, method, commandments and or judgment of God is potentially dangerous and hazardous. For those who just must see things their way, I challenge you to reconsider who you are debating with. Surely a rational believer will concede that our thought process is inferior to God's. For our way is not His way, neither are our thoughts.

Most times we spend more time qualifying the messenger than the message. Sometime the message is believable, but we are so critical of the credentials and qualifications of the messenger we again refuse to believe. How many times have you heard or even said yourself,

Blessed With Less

"that individual can't tell me anything"? Sometimes they are credible, yet we contest anyway. Moses was undeniably one of the greatest leaders in history. The children of Israel watched him contend with pharaoh. They were with him, when, at his word plagues came and went. He led millions from bondage, out of Egypt. They watched him part the Red Sea. Nations witnessed his personal relationship with "The God of Israel". However, multitudes malingered, murmured, debated and contended with his directions and decisions. There was so much resistance that it took them forty years to walk a less than two-week journey.

Imagine there were two (2) men, and you had previous knowledge of these following factual characteristics: the 1st has multiple prejudices; in that he was a bigot and a racist. He was also a drug dealing, drug using thief and a robber. In addition, he was also a homosexual, pedophile. The 2nd man was a vegetarian, drank an occasional social beer, never had any known infidelity and didn't like the way politicians were handling the countries affairs, so he put in his bid to become a world leader. That 1st man proceeds to use profane and derogatory language toward your child and you because in his opinion both of you are ignorant and racially inferior. In his yelling, he adds if you're not too stupid to understand the English language, get your child out of the street because a truck is coming. How do you respond? Do you ignore him and tell the child to follow suit? Will you be so caught up with the presentation of the message that you miss or dismiss the actual point? In contrast, the 2nd man who appears nice is now identified as Adolph Hitler. How relevant is bio of either man at that moment?

Chapter 3 Pride, Doubt, Frustration

Indulge me by reviewing your opinion based on the presentation of the following 2-page, 2-part poem entitled:
"The Doomed" *By: The ≠ Poet Joel*
This can become our reality if we don't change it

<u>"The Doomed"</u>

We are Doomed
I refuse to believe
God Made a way over 2000 years ago
This may be a rude awakening but
"Happiness comes from within"
Is a lie, and
"money will make you happy"
I will teach my children and grands
They are not the most important thing in my
life
My job and boss will know that
I have my priority straight
Work
Is more important than
Family
and
my Family
is
God whom I worship

Blessed With Less

"The Doomed" (*Cont'd*)

I tell you this
We teach of a risen savior
this will not be true in my era
Christianity is dead
Experts say
I do not concede
We will live without doubt or fear
In the future
Hate and degradation will be the norm
No Longer can it be said
The Church cares about all people
It will be clear that
we live in a faithless and perverse time
There are no righteous and
My generation sins continually
It is ridiculous to believe
There is Hope !

Everything is based on perception and understanding.
Now that you've formed an opinion, read the next 2 pages:

The Doomed Reversed

There is Hope !
It is ridiculous to believe
My generation sins continually
There are no righteous and
we live in a faithless and perverse time
It will be clear that
The Church cares about all people
No Longer can it be said
Hate and degradation will be the norm
In the future
We will live without doubt or fear
I do not concede
Experts say
Christianity is dead
this will not be true in my era
We teach of a risen savior
I tell you this
God whom I worship

The Doomed Reversed *(Cont'd)*

is
my Family
and
Family
Is more important than
Work
I have my priority straight
My job and boss will know that
They are not the most important thing in my life
I will teach my children and grands
"money will make you happy"
Is a lie, and
"Happiness comes from within"
This may be a rude awakening but
God Made a way 2000 years ago
I refuse to believe
We are Doomed

This is what happens with change!

Chapter 3 Pride, Doubt, Frustration

After seeing the same exact words presented in the same complete sentences can you honestly say you hold the same opinion? Perspective is subjective, but it is still up to you to look beyond what seems obvious and sometimes even logical and just believe. Doubt causes us to question and then debate almost everything. From the simplest thought dealing with creation, the questions are now common. How did we come into being? When does, life begin, at conception or later? Which came first the chicken or the egg? Can you imagine the confusion and the length of debate when it was first mentioned the earth just might be round? I can imagine God looking at us the way the first version of the poem was written; all the right words but presented backwards. How many times have we done the right thing the wrong way ? A condescending, back-handed compliment.

We say we want the truth, answers and even help, but I've seen many instances where help was refused based on the race or religion of the person offering the help. In all fairness, sometimes we just don't want to be viewed as gullible. However, most times we plainly refuse to give anyone the benefit of the doubt. Our biases cause us to believe a lie rather than accept the truth. The U.S.A. still recognizes a paid federal holiday the 2nd Monday in October. Pride says Columbus discovered America; doubt says that civilized people could not have been living here already. The frustration is knowing the truth and not liking it.

Oh, the pain of frustration. Angry that things aren't going our way. Too much pride to own the responsibility and too much doubt to believe the answer. Too much pride to ask for or receive the answer. Frustrated that someone who we deem less qualified than us is providing a solution. The frustration of having so much pride that we can't accept someone other than ourselves receiving any accolades or even credit. Frustration will cause us to make hasty, erratic decisions. Frustrated that we can't get anything done. Eventually facts prove that we couldn't get anything done because we were frustrated. That frustration is stressful, and stress kills. Sometimes just talking to someone; get things off your chest reduces stress. But you probably doubt they could help you. Even if you thought they could your pride won't allow you to be open with anyone. Warning in less than half of an average lifetime you will self-destruct. However, consider the possibilities if you'd put your pride aside, doubt less, consider other opinions, try to accept them and not complain, you'll be less frustrated and positioned to be blessed.

THERE

IS

HOPE

Do The Math

$$\begin{array}{rl} & \text{FAITH} \\ + & \text{WORKS} \\ - & \text{DOUBT} \\ \hline = & \text{SALVATION} \end{array}$$

Chapter 4

Praise,
Practice,
Contentment

Praise is the opposite of criticizing or condemning. When we are not praising we are usually expressing ourselves by complaining. Even without speaking, our posture and very persona changes. We have frowns, we roll our eyes, we move slower, dragging our feet, our shoulders droop, we slump and or we sigh in exacerbation. Praise in Latin is Pretium which in the literal, translates into Price. In old French, it's Preisier which means prize and then transforms into praise. That is where we get our now common term appraisal. We are actually placing a value on our complement. In the English translation praise means to pay tribute or speak highly of. Praise is to compliment, congratulate, hail, applaud, adore and or depending on the specific circumstances, eulogize.

Personally, I don't know any individual who doesn't appreciate being praised, even if only a little. There are several ways to express praise, both verbal and non-verbal. However, most everyone wants to audibly hear some form of approval for whatever they have done; even when it's something they were supposed to do. Quite honestly, it's an exceptionally good feeling when people are speaking well of you. Even when a person is deceased, the family and friends take time and make a concerted effort to ensure that good things are said about that individual. You hardly ever hear of a funeral where anyone gets up to speak and says negative things about the deceased. In fact, most times that person is pronounced to have made their peace with God and is declared to be "in a better place". The masses believe that person is looking down on us from a heavenly place with God. That type of memorial service is referred to as a "home going service" as opposed to a funeral.

Although most have difficulty praising someone else, we will go through great lengths assuming a gregarious posture and mentality, to gain approval from others who most times are not even worthy. Many are extreme in their attempt to obtain attention; historically and statically this behavior is predominately attributed to females. The insatiable desire to hear that famous three-word phrase, "I Love You". However, they will settle for hearing positive references such as attractive, pretty, beautiful, lovely, cute or drop dead gorgeous. Even if it's not true, those terms of endearment are considered normal and acceptable behavior; then there are the exceptionally egregious. The American Psychiatric Association noted that "histrionic personality disorder" (HPD) is a disorder characterized by a pattern of excessive "attention-seeking" emotions. This behavior is usually seen in early adulthood, and includes inappropriate seductive behavior and an excessive need for approval. Some may not have a personality disorder, but rather a social or etiquette deficiency, in that they will accept and even encourage vulgar, lude and even derogatory or negative comments as compliments. No matter who you are, whether your desire to hear compliments is considered normal or a disorder; it is better to give (compliments) than to receive; Especially when you are giving to one who deserves accolades or praise.

Who then is worthy of praise? In the U.S.A. we are taught to honor and praise our mothers more than any other individual. Even when mothers aren't good mothers, we are still reminded that "you only get one mother". We are further instructed to at the very least, give her honor and praise if only because she carried you full term. Growing up mothers were off limits. If you spoke about anyone's mother, even in jest, you better had been prepared to fight. After mothers come children. Support them, encourage them, find a way to compliment them. Many children have been misguided because someone was so afraid of hurting their feelings, or they loved them so much they were blind to their disruptive, destructive behavior. Seldom do you hear the masses earnestly encourage honoring father.

As a society, we accept the concept of honoring supporting and praising our local athletes and respective teams. However, in contrast, when it comes to the opposing team, we yell all types of negative comments referencing them. We will desecrate and even burn their uniform, or a semblance thereof. But our favorite and or the "popular" team; we'll wear their team colors, shirts, hats and jackets, for sports we have never played ourselves. We learn their theme song or music and chant their names. Even if they are the worse team in their league, there are still die-hard fans that will continue to support and encourage them. And if they win, the bragging rights begin. We put bumper stickers on our cars, flags and banners in our windows, memorabilia on our shelves and ringtones on our phones. Furthermore, we have award ceremonies for actors and artists, for performing. People who put on a persona, or outright pretend to be something and or someone they are not. All this to praise people we have never met and who don't know us; and in all probability, could care less if they ever met us.

Every now and then a local hero will arise. Often, it's an ordinary civilian who happened to be in a specific place at a specific time and responded appropriately. Sometimes all they did was place a call for help. Then there are those who go above and beyond, putting themselves in harm's way, to help others. Several civil servants place their lives on the line every day to protect the freedom and liberty of others. Seldom does a civic leader show up, but when they do, great is the impact. Unfortunately, they are usually first met with great opposition, critical analysis and even accusations; which ironically ultimately help us to recognize their greatness. Surely these individuals are worthy of some level of honor. Sadly, that acknowledgment, most times doesn't occur until after they are dead.

Many are still receiving credit and compensation for the accomplishments of others. Friends, relatives and associates obtain fame, fortune and perpetual residual income for the inventions of others. This great nation financed a war gaining its independence with free labor from minorities, and to this day "they" still will not, as a collective people, acknowledge the input of those same minorities. That is those who are in power, those that have authority and even the so-called common folks. Not even the veterans who gave their lives for this country receive the same benefits. Their compensation varies, based on their individual race, religion and political affiliation. There are leaders such as Martin Luther King jr. and Harriet Tubman that have received global recognition for their efforts, yet there are groups and even states who protest any form of formal honor. Even animals have advocates, demanding that animals be recognized, appreciated and provided for. Are you aware if you harm or God forbid kill a Police Dog or Horse, "under the Federal Law Enforcement Animal Protection Act" you will be charged with committing a crime against an "officer" of the law. This felony charge carries a penalty, which is: a fine of at least one thousand dollars ($1,000.00) and spending up to ten years in prison. Yet unarmed minorities are killed regularly but seldom is a penalty imposed on the individual murderer. Eventually after marches, protests and petitions by activists, a settlement of some form of compensation may be rendered. How does one compensate for a life, exactly what is the value of a human life? In one light, we go on a tangent excessively praising and honoring and even idolizing humans and on the other hand we diminish their importance by recognizing animals more than human life. The extreme epitome of those who "worshipped and served the creature more than the creator" (Romans 1:25). I am aware that this scripture is talking about humans worshipping humans, but how much more demeaning and disrespectful is it to reverence or value an animal more?

Chapter 4 Praise, Practice, Contentment

Unfortunately, this mentality is not new, in the Gospel of Matthew 12:9-14 Jesus encountered some likeminded individuals, in that He was being condemned for healing a man on the Sabbath. However, Jesus immediately showed them their selves by asking if they would not lift one of their fallen sheep out of a pit on any given Sabbath. Then He emphatically declared that a human life was much better than a sheep's. I am in no way shape or form suggesting or promoting any form of inhumane treatment, cruelty or abuse of an animal. However, I am stating we need to value human life and that can be done without any reference or resemblance to worshipping a human being. It's amazing knowing that if you told only the acts of many humans, without divulging the participant's identity, sex, race or religion, the majority would agree that respect and even reverence is due. We go through battles, protests, litigations and even wars for animals and humans with limitations; how much more should we praise the creator.

God has unlimited capabilities and has done more for us collectively and individually than any other, yet we are apprehensive about giving Him His due. Some have used as an excuse that God has everything, doesn't need anything and there is nothing we can give to Him. However, Revelation 4:11 declares "Thou art worthy, O Lord, to receive glory, and honour and power: for thou hast created all things, and for thy pleasure they are and were created". Preceding that King David, knowing the importance, gave some specific assignments, namely: "And He appointed certain of the Levites to minister before the ark of the Lord, and to record, and to thank and praise the Lord God of Israel" 1st Chronicles 16:4. He continued by asking: "What profit is there in my blood, when I go down to the pit? Shall the dust praise thee? Shall it declare thy truth?" Psalm 30:9. He clearly understood that mankind was made to praise God. There are many forms and manners in which this command can successfully be performed. There is both direct and indirect praise. Just think of the praise we give mothers for their participation in a natural child birth. Have you ever considered who gave her the ability to conceive, carry and deliver? I'm not trivializing nor diminishing the role of a mother, but we need to learn perspective. We buy mothers candy, flowers, cards, jewelry, cars, vacations and even homes. Most mature mothers are appreciative but express to their children the sentiment: more than anything tangible, they want your love, respect and obedience. God wants, deserves and requires the same and more.

King David gave this affirmation: "I was glad when they said unto me let us go into the house of the Lord." (Psalm 122:1) He was glad for the mere opportunity and invitation. Followed by his personal commitment saying, "I will bless the Lord at all times: His praise shall continually be in my mouth" (Psalm 34:1). Then he admonished others saying; "oh that men would praise the Lord for his goodness, and for his wonderful works to the children of men"! On another occasion he encouraged a corporate collective praise saying: "O magnify the Lord with me, and let us exalt His name together" (Psalm 34:3). He gave instruction for his personal, other individuals and groups. Some curiously ask; how and what can we give to God? This is not an option, we can, should, and are further commanded, to give unto God through our praise. Psalm 150 puts it in this manner:

150:1 "Praise ye the Lord. Praise God in his sanctuary: praise Him in the firmament of His power.

150:2 Praise Him for His might acts: praise Him according to His excellent greatness.

150:3 Praise Him with the sound of the trumpet: praise Him with the psaltery and harp.

150: 4 Praise Him with timbrel and dance: praise Him with stringed instruments and organs.

150: 5 Praise Him upon the loud cymbals: praise Him upon the high-sounding cymbals.

150:6 Let everything that hath breath praise the Lord. Praise ye the Lord".

This psalm emphasizes and details many forms of praise. Its opening sentence first and foremost commands us to at bare minimum, Praise. It continues by telling us who to praise, which is, the Lord. It tells us what to praise Him for, (His mighty acts) and continues telling us what to praise Him with. It details the utilization of various musical instruments. It tells us to also praise Him with a dance. Then it definitively, and collectively without exception commands everything that has breath to praise the Lord. This praise is a physical expression carried out in many ways. We can bless, exalt, extol, magnify and glorify His name. We can shabach, which is a loud shout denoting triumph. Like the crowd at a sporting event or concert. Tehillah; which means to sing. Todah is to extend your hands, in a hailing manner. Yadah is to extend or thrust your hands, like during a competitive chant while rooting for an athlete; but Yada in Hebrew means to know. Yes, you can praise God by knowing, understanding and learning about Him. Noting that most only seek to earnestly learn about someone that they admire. Kara means to dance. We are not casually or trivially saying thank you, but with everything in us and that which we have access to, we are deliberately presenting it to God with joy and excitement.

We who claim to be people of God should strive to be praise practitioners. A practitioner is one who has a professional practice or job, such as a law practice, but it is most often used when referring to a medical professional. This type of practice differs drastically from a mere rehearsal, ritual or religion, in that here one strives for a level of excellence or form of perfection. People who participate in a ritual or form of religion tend to have a mundane complacency about themselves and in the manner in which they do things. Almost like an unconscious habit or mannerism as opposed to a conscious deliberate endeavor. There should be a concerted effort on our part to intentionally practice with earnest praise every day. Praising God, not haphazardly, nor out of convenience, but daily in all that we say and or do. Colossians 3:17 states "Whatsoever ye do in word or deed, do all in the name of the Lord Jesus, giving thanks to God the Father by Him".

There are also more passive ways to praise, which still contains a physical posture, but more subtle. This is when we are settled in whatever is going on around us or even in us. It is a contentment that simply says all is well. The kind of posture we see when a parent or companion may not be able to perform in a big way. When they can't afford an expensive gift, but you assure them that it doesn't matter. When your living conditions aren't extravagant, but you can still say "as long as we are together" it's okay. That is the type of contentment we must have with God. Believing in Him and knowing that He is able to do all things but accepting that if He doesn't, it is well with us. Sometimes all we need to do is smile while we are dealing with our situation as opposed to looking like we are sorry we were ever born. Or worse verbalizing our disappointment with how God dealt with us. This is unfathomable for some, but the three well known Hebrew boys, Hananiah (Shadrach), Mishael (Meshach), and Azariah (Abed-nego, maintained this positive position. First non-verbally, but when asked; with confidence boldness and determination, they said: "our God whom we serve is able to deliver us from the burning fiery furnace, and He will deliver us out of thine hand, O king. But if not, be it know unto thee, O king that we will not serve thy gods, nor worship the golden image which thou hast set up" (Daniel 3:17-18).

We must recognize that He is God, besides Him there is no other. "It is He that hath made us and not we ourselves" (Psalm 100:3). The same way we applaud our favorite athlete for giving us a professional, championship performance, we should acknowledge God. Even more so, because God is not seasonal; more so, just because He's God. The same way we are satisfied when our child gives their best effort, we should appreciate God. God gives us His best effort without failure every day. The same way we reverence a mother for carrying us full term, we must reverence and thank God for creation. The same way most mothers tell you that they are your mother on more than just "Mother's Day", Christmas and or their Birthday.

Blessed With Less

Every living, breathing creature owes God their praise. No matter what your age, gender, color, height, weight or status, there are no exceptions. Whether you are Blond, brunette, redhead or bald. Whether your eye color is black, brown, blue, green or hazel. Whether you are near-sighted, far-sighted or blind; whether you have 20-20 vision or have no eyes at all. If you are still alive you owe and should be willing to give God praise "The dead praise not, the Lord, neither any that go down into silence". (Psalm 115:17) Especially if you are professing to be a faithful servant of God. "Praise is comely for the upright" (Psalm 33:1). Comely is pleasant to look at; agreeable and suitable for those who are living in compliance to God's standards. We are the ones who know emphatically that God is good and greatly to be praised.

Praise is not a suggestion; it is a command. Praise is something we should practice regularly. It amazes me that serious professions like Law and medicine are considered and called "a practice". I don't know anyone in any sport or craft that doesn't practice. They do this with the intent of getting better, how much more should we strive to offer, "perfect praise". Praise is written in the King James version of the Bible a total of two hundred and forty-eight (248) times; two hundred and twenty-two (222) in the old testament and twenty-six (26) times in the new. Any Noun or verb written that many times must have great significance. In Psalm 148 explains that everything in the heavens and in the earth, was created to praise. We should "enter into His gates with thanksgiving, and into His courts with praise; be thankful unto Him, and bless His name. for the Lord is Good; His mercy is everlasting; and His truth endureth to all generations" (Psalm 100:4-5). Even those who are called misfortunate or are seen in a negative light are still obligated to praise God. "O let not the oppressed return ashamed: let the poor and needy praise thy name" (Psalm 74:21). It is this collective posture, practice and ability that we should carry out with contentment. Continually humbling ourselves and praising God; that constitutes us being blessed.

PRAISE GOD Despite FEAR
PRACTICE Makes Perfect, FACT
CONTENTMENT is a Rewarding FEELING

Chapter 5

Fear,
Facts,
Feelings

There is nothing to fear but fear itself. A paraphrase of a famous line used in the 1933 inaugural address of Franklin D. Roosevelt. It sounds simple enough, so why and what do so many people fear. Some fear simply based on their personal feelings; their emotions. I heard Will Smith state in his movie "After Earth": "fear is not real, it is a product of the thoughts we create, don't get me wrong, Danger is real, Fear is a choice". Why does one fear, do we really have a choice?

I've discovered this is not one dimensional, but varies; most are afraid of the unknown. They have no idea why they are afraid. Others are afraid because they legitimately have facts to substantiate their thoughts. But where do they get these facts, where do they get these thoughts? Some researchers took the time to name and compile a list our every fear under the title of phobias. Note: a phobia is an extreme or irrational fear of or aversion to something. It is a form of fear, which overwhelms your mind and shakes your confidence. It causes you to lack the courage to face situations in life. Although the number grows every day, there are currently hundreds of know phobias. However, they are categorically broken down and classified into three distinct groups.

Chapter 5 Fear, Facts, Feelings

1). **<u>Social phobia</u>** is just as it sounds; you are afraid of being socially disgraced or mortified. You are uncomfortable talking or even being seen in public.

2). **<u>Specific Phobia</u>** is limited to the specific object, entity or place. This can be as trivial as a particular insect, an altitude such as height (planes and tall buildings), depth (underground subway and oceans) or a tight or close space (elevator). You can even have a phobia of something natural and needful to live (like water).

3). **<u>Agoraphobia</u>** is a fear of being trapped unable to escape a place or situation. This condition is also referred to as a fear of public places. It is common for an individual to have more than one phobia at the same time. Often phobias overlap and become very confusing to the individual and anyone they meet, especially if the observer thinks it's an unwarranted, unnecessary overreaction. Because you can be afraid of almost anything I don't believe the list will ever end. However, I am currently aware of over five hundred (500) phobias that exist. Below denoting both the name and description, is an extensive alphabetized list of a little over one hundred (100) phobias:

A

Ablutophobia	Fear of washing or bathing
Achluophobia	Fear of darkness
Acrophobia	**Fear of heights**
Aerophobia	**Fear of flying**
Agoraphobia	**Fear of open spaces or crowds**
Agyrophobia	Fear of crossing the street
Aichmophobia	Fear of needles or pointed objects
Algophobia	Fear of pain
Amaxophobia	Fear of riding in a car

Blessed With Less

Androphobia	Fear of men
Anginophobia	Fear of angina or choking
Anthrophobia	Fear of flowers
Anthropophobia	Fear of people or society
Aphenphosmphobia	Fear of being touched
Arachnophobia	**Fear of spiders**
Arithmophobia	Fear of numbers
Astraphobia	Fear of thunder and lightning
Ataxophobia	Fear of disorder or untidiness
Atelophobia	Fear of imperfection
Atychiphobia	Fear of failure
Autophobia	Fear of being alone

B

Bacteriophobia	Fear of Bacteria
Barophobia	Fear of gravity
Bathmophobia	Fear of stairs or steep slopes
Batrachophobia	Fear of amphibians
Belonephobia	Fear of pins and needles
Bibliophobia	Fear of books
Botanophobia	Fear of plants

C

Cacophobia	Fear of ugliness
Catagelophobia	Fear of being ridiculed
Catoptrophobia	Fear of mirrors
Chionophobia	Fear of snow
Chromophobia	Fear of colors
Chronomentrophobia	Fear of clocks
Claustrophobia	Fear of confined spaces
Coulrophobia	Fear of clowns
Cyberphobia	Fear of computers
Cynophobia	Fear of dogs

D

Decidophobia	Fear of making decisions
Dendrophobia	Fear of trees
Dentophobia	**Fear of dentists**
Domatophobia	Fear of houses
Dystychiphobia	Fear of accidents

E

Ecophobia	Fear of the home
Elurophobia	Fear of cats
Entomophobia	Fear of insects
Ephebiphobia	Fear of teenagers
Equinophobia	Fear of horses

F

Febriphobia	Fear of fever (spelling 1 of 3)
Felinophobia	Fear of cats
Fibriphobia	Fear of fever (spelling 2 of 3)
Fibriophobia	Fear of fever (spelling 3 of 3)
Frigophobia	Fear of cold or cold things

G

Gamophobia	**Fear of marriage**
Genuphobia	Fear of knees
Glossophobia	Fear of speaking in public
Gynophobia	Fear of women

H

Heliophobia	Fear of the sun
Hemophobia	**Fear of blood**
Herpetophobia	Fear of reptiles
Hydrophobia	Fear of water
Hypochonria	**Fear of illness**

Blessed With Less

I

Iatrophobia   **Fear of doctors**
Insectophobia   Fear of insects

K

Kainolophobia   Fear of anything new, novelty
Koinoniphobia   Fear of rooms

L

Leukophobia   Fear of the color white
Lilapsophobia   Fear of tornadoes and hurricanes
Lockiophobia   Fear of childbirth

M

Mageirocophobia   Fear of cooking
Megalophobia   Fear of large things
Melanophobia   **Fear of the color black**
Microphobia   Fear of small things
Mysophobia   Fear of dirt and germs

N

Necrophobia   Fear of death or dead things
Noctiphobia   Fear of the night
Nosocomephobia   Fear of hospitals
Nyctophobia   Fear of the dark

O

Obesophobia   Fear of gaining weight
Ochlophobia   Fear of crowd or mobs
Octophobia   Fear of the figure 8
Ombrophobia   Fear of rain
Ophidiophobia   **Fear of snakes**
Ornithophobia   **Fear of birds**

P

Papyrophobia	Fear of paper
Pathophobia	Fear of disease
Pedophobia	Fear of children
Philematophobia	Fear of kissing
Philophobia	Fear of **love**
Phobophobia	Fear of phobias
Podophobia	Fear of feet
Porphyrophobia	Fear of the color purple
Pteridophobia	Fear of ferns
Pteromerhanophobia	Fear of flying
Pyrophobia	Fear of fire

S

Samhainophobia	Fear of Halloween
Scolionophobia	Fear of school
Scopophobia	Fear of being seen or stared at
Scotophobia	Fear of darkness
Selenophobia	Fear of the moon
Sociophobia	Fear of social evaluation
Somniphobia	Fear of sleep
Sophophobia	**Fear of Learning**

T

Tachophobia	Fear of speed
Technophobia	Fear of technology
Thalassophobia	Fear of the ocean
Tonitrophobia	Fear of thunder
Trichophobia	Fear of hair
Tridecaphobia	Fear of the number thirteen
Trypanophobia	Fear of needles / injections
Trypophobia	Fear of holes.

Blessed With Less

V

Venustraphobia	Fear of beautiful women
Verminophobia	Fear of germs

W

Wiccaphobia	Fear of witches and witchcraft

X

Xenophobia	Fear of strangers or foreigners

Z

Zeusophobia	**Fear of God or gods**
Zoophobia	Fear of animals

While I agree that in most cases, we can choose whether we are afraid, I also believe we should not ignore an existing known fear. Whether it is our fear or the fear belonging to some we know or maybe even casually meet. Fear is an unpleasant emotion caused by the belief that someone or something is dangerous, likely to cause pain, or a threat. Some people are taught to be afraid, generally by someone who has fears themselves. However, fear is also introduced and imposed by oppressors, who will taunt, and play with and on your emotions. They will threaten you or a loved one to get you to comply, and perpetually "keep you in line". The threat varies based on what that perpetrator believes will work on you. While some may be threatened with bodily harm, others need that threat to be directed at their loved ones. During slavery, the "masters" would threaten to sell or separate the spouse or child of a non-compliant or hostile slave. In this day and time, the threat is somewhat reversed, where an individual is being manipulated with the fear of their companion leaving them. Still another may be extorted by the fear of exposure. This could be something true or a lie that an extortionist spreads, either way the result could be catastrophically devastating for most. Illegal immigrants have been coerced to work for below minimum wage rates, for fear of being reported and potentially deported. Even those with legitimate jobs, are the requests / demands imposed by employers reasonable and obtainable; or are they scare tactics?

Fear can cause us to act in an irrational manner. The response of a fearful person varies drastically. One may cower and hide in fear, while another may kill everyone in sight, yet another may commit suicide, all from the same fear. The fact is the threat may be real, but the response is up to you. I guess that then depends on how you feel about the implied threat. Have you ever said or heard someone say, "I have a bad feeling about this"? What or who are you afraid of, what fear or threat or feeling will you concede to?

According to a study conducted by Elizabeth Kubler Ross, "There are only two emotions: love and fear. All positive emotions come from love, all negative emotions from fear. From love flows happiness, contentment, peace, and joy. From fear comes anger, hate, anxiety, and guilt. It's true that there are only two primary emotions, love and fear. But it's more accurate to say that there is only love and fear, for we cannot feel these two emotions together, at exactly the same time. They're opposites. If we're in fear, we are not in a place of love. When we're in a place of love, we cannot be in a place of fear." Mrs. Ross was the oldest of triplets born, 1926 in Zurich Switzerland; was raised as a Protestant Christian

Blessed With Less

and studied Psychiatry. She. moved to New York City, USA in 1958, where she continued and extended her education. In 2007 Mrs. Ross was inducted into the American National Women's Hall of Fame. She is noted as a pioneer in near-death studies, encouraging hospice care and the author of the book: "On Death and Dying" (1969).

I refuse to base my life solely on emotions, science, psychology or philosophy; but on the truth of God's word, which happens to agree with the findings of this study. "There is no fear in love; but perfect love casteth out fear: because fear hath torment. He that feareth is not made perfect in love" (1st John 4:18). I have resolved the only one that should be feared is God. Not with apprehension or trepidation, rather in awe. "The fear of the Lord is the beginning of wisdom; but fools despise wisdom and instruction" (Proverbs 1:7). God is not a terrorist. "For God hath not given us the spirit of fear, but of power and of love and of a sound mind." (1st Timothy 1:7. If we be children of God, whom shall we fear. In contrast, those who should fear are noted in Revelation 21:8 "But the fearful, and the unbelieving, and the abominable, and murderers, and whoremongers, and sorcerers, and idolaters, and all liars, shall have their part in the lake which burneth with fire and brimstone: which is the second death".

I'm sure some "formal educators will no doubt have a problem with this next statement, yet I am compelled to present it. I know the general teaching is that emotions and feelings cannot be measured, but facts can, and therefore said facts can be proof of truth. However, I contend that all facts do not in and of its independent self, constitute truth.

Chapter 5 Fear, Facts, Feelings

Documents can be misinterpreted and or manipulated, thus leading to judgements based on misinformation. Content taken out of context produces misconduct. The truth of the matter is, most truths cannot clearly be documented, thus dispelling the proof needed to substantiate it as a fact. In accordance with God's standard, if you are not operating in the spirit, you're in the flesh, which are your feelings. Those feelings if based on reality and facts alone can cause you to fear. This next noted fact may have social conflicts but 'm sure it contains a perspective to consider. "Caitlyn Jenner" is legally a woman; however the "full" truth is that same individual was born a male child named "Bruce Jenner". If you only based on the facts you are in for a rude awakening and that in my opinion is something to fear.

In general, the people who usually don't fear are children, the ignorant and Worshippers of God. Noting that children are unaware of the dangers they are confronted with and ignorant only means lacking knowledge or uninformed. Because of their lack of information, or as in the case of a child, the lack of knowledge that there is something to fear, they tend to have a false sense of security. But for the worshipper we make this statement in a rhetorical question form; "The Lord is my light and my salvation, whom shall I fear? The Lord is the strength of my life, of whom shall I be afraid?" (Psalms 27:1) Thus our faith overrides our fear. We clearly being fully informed of the dangers we face, rely on our faith and continue.

"Let us hear the conclusion of the whole matter; Fear God, and keep His commandments; for this is the whole duty of man" (Ecclesiastes 12:13). The facts may say I have a condition, or situation, my feelings may even concur, but my faith says: "Though an host should encamp against me, my heart shall not fear; though war should rise against me, in this will I be confident" (Psalms 27:3). Those wars could be literal or metaphoric. They could be physical, emotional, financial, psychological or spiritual. They may be as real as real can be; as opposed to a figment of my imagination. However, I refuse to allow my problems or situations to appear to be bigger, greater or more powerful than my God. I am more than a mere praiser, I am a worshipper. Anyone and everything can praise God, but a worshipper has a different relationship.

The scripture made a clear distinction saying: "Ye are of your father the devil, and the lusts of your father ye will do" (John 8:44). I, being righteous, have the right to call God my Father. And I stand firm that my Father can beat any other father. To the believer this assurance is written: "And ye shall hear of wars and rumors of wars: see that ye be not troubled: for all these things must come to pass, but the end is not yet" (Matthew 24:6). The combination of the two terms "fear not" and "do not be afraid" are written in the Bible three hundred sixty-five (365) times. Therefore, the less I subscribe to my feelings, the less afraid I will be. Feelings are emotions that change frequently. The less I subscribe to the technicality of facts, the more opportunity to exercise my faith and when I need reassurance I can find a different scripture to encourage me every single day of the year. The knowledgeable lack of fear is a strong sign of belief. That much belief and confidence in the giver of all blessings, puts me that much closer to being blessed.

POWER
WITHOUT AUTHORITY
IS TYRANNY

Chapter 6

Power,
Authority,
Dominion

"Absolute power corrupts absolutely" is the best-known quotation of the 19th century British politician, Lord Acton. It is noted that he "borrowed" the idea from several other writers who had previously expressed the same thought. Noting that some of the best men when given too much power tend to become corrupt, some even became so heady they thought they were some form of god. So what is power? Power as a noun is defined as: the ability to do something or act in a particular way, especially as a faculty or quality. However, in physics it is the amount of energy put out or produced in a given amount of time. If we were to account for the ambiguity, the full definition is the ability to act or produce an effect. 2. Capacity for being acted upon or undergoing effect. Legal or official authority, capacity or right. And as a verb it is simply supply.

Although there are several, I will first concentrate on social power, because it is animated and deals with human behavior. There are five sources of social power we need to address, and they are as follows: coercive, expert, legitimate, referent, and reward. Coercive power is: the ability to influence someone's decision by taking something away as punishment or the threat of punishment.

Chapter 6 Power, Authority, Dominion

With coercive power, one uses leverage to coerce or sway an individual or group to act, perform, or vote in a certain manner or direction. It is the method used as manipulative motivation of lax employees and or in sometime necessary extreme discipline, even to the threat of the loss of a job. Often this type is viewed negatively, like when used in blackmail or extortion.

Expert power is based on the subordinate employee's perception that a manager or relevant superior, or even one with seniority has a high level of knowledge or a specialized set of skills that the other employees or members of said organization do not possess. The individuals or groups who concede to those who they believe know more, are usually docile or compliant therefore more easily manageable. Although this is a logical form of deduction often we must qualify the possessor of said perceived or even noted knowledge and ensure that it's tailored to our specific situation before we follow. At least with expert power said individual does know something about the working order of whatever they are trying to lord over. However, their effectiveness or success rate might not hold the same weight as perceived by a subordinate. Often said superior is drifting on a memory of a positive standing from the past and may not currently be up to speed.

Legitimate power is power derived from a formal position or office held in the organization's hierarchy of authority. Note just because a person has legitimate power does not mean they deserve such a position. However, they were legally granted or possibly inherited said position, be-it a supervisor, manager, CEO or even owner. Nonetheless, that individual is the heir with all rights, privileges, power and authority. An individual with legitimate power who is aware of their inept ability, if wise, will surround themselves with qualified capable supporters and delegate full responsibility to them.

Referent power refers to the ability of a leader to influence a follower because of the follower's loyalty, respect, friendship, admiration, affection or desire to gain approval. This is used so frequently in each of our everyday lives, sometimes so subtle it is undetected. This power is one of the easiest to abuse and therefore must be handled with extreme care by both parties. It is commonly and frequently used by couples, parents, siblings, spiritual leaders and most anyone with any type of longevity or seniority. It is an unearned, and in many cases undeserved sense of entitlement based mostly on an emotional attachment. Generally, this is based on the time one has in a particular place and very little to do with any accomplishments. They clearly had just been there without going against the grain. Sometimes they are just the oldest person in the area so the inherently were granted a senior position.

Reward power is power conveyed through rewarding individuals for compliance with one's wishes. This is in all probability the simplest and generally most motivating for the subordinate. Most often equated as the exact opposite of coercive, in that it incentivizes and is seen in a positive light. The possessor of this power gives promotions raises, time off from work and bonuses. The danger is it could be perceived as a sign of weakness for the authority issuing the reward. One could argue that those with reward power attempt to buy loyalty or bribe workers, instead of giving orders. It is also noted that subordinates are not genuinely concerned about the good working order, but are only interested in how much they can be rewarded.

While power, authority, and dominion have each frequently been used interchangeably, there is a distinct independent difference between the three. Some of the synonyms we associate with power are: strength, might, force, influence, knowledge, ability, competence, money, dominance control, command and awe. However, the definitions also equate with dominion and authority. There is personal power which you possess on your own, allocated power which is given to you in portions and position power which could be given but something you also can take by force. Personal power may be exhibited in many forms. That power can be Physical, emotional, mental, financial, social political and or spiritual.

Water is said to be one of the most powerful natural sources on earth. It at one time was attributed to the destruction of all life as we know it except for one family and the animals they collected and secured in an ark. Fire is destructively powerful; however, water can put fire out. Water is so strong it has carved caves, tunnels and valleys in and through mountains. Even when not in full force, water will through persistence find its way through cracks and crevices so small they are undetectable to the human eye. It is no mere coincidence that the earth and the human body are both made up of approximately seventy-five percent (75%) water; giving more credence to the fact that the human body contains the components of earth from which it was made.

Blessed With Less

Most people have a small purport and or form of power, authority and or dominion. Those that have more, or multiple facets of power generally aren't aware of all they possess. Moreover, none have full governing control independent of themselves. I know we all must answer to the ultimate sovereign power of God, but I am in fact talking about natural human power. If your only component of power is your personal physical muscle strength, then, more often than not, someone with another variation of power will control you; be it mental, physical, position, financial or political.

You could have all the strength and even the ability to use it, but in order to effectively operate you still need the authority to do so. Likewise, you may have the authority but now need someone with the ability to perform that which you are authorized to do. A 5' tall 95lb elderly woman wearing a school crossing guard uniform, can stand in front of a big rig, eighteen-wheel truck, which averages 30,000 pounds' empty. Although the truck is bigger, stronger and is driven by someone with ability, if operating legally they now must yield and be subject to the authority. The president of the United States of America is the commander in chief of the combined U.S. Armed forces. When he wants a city, region or country subdued, does he personally physically ball up his fists and fight or fire a weapon. His authority dictates what should be done, when and where. He has dominion over his domain and subsequently whatever domain he conquers. He exerts his legitimate authoritative power, gives an order, and subordinates carry out those orders.

Dominion is defined as control but equates with supremacy, superiority, command, rule, jurisdiction and sovereignty. How is dominion obtained one might ask? Based on one ethnicity, specific location, color, religion, political affiliation, culture and or the time, this could vary drastically. In 1491 it was probably a good year to be a Native American Indian, but in 1942 that changed. July 1776 was a great time to be an American, ironically prior to that date we didn't even exist as a nation, but now we acquired our own domain. In 1985 the 1st registered internet domain, although not the 1st created was "Symbolics". That ".com" entity was formed four years before the "worldwide Webb existed. They claimed rites to an area no one was using, cornering a market. In 1993 Symbolics filed for bankruptcy and was subsequently sold; hence noting that some domains can and will continue to be bought and sold, or taken over.

There are three domains of learning: Cognitive, Affective, and Psychomotor. Cognitive domain is the development of mental abilities. This includes comprehension, retention, perception and psychological application. in short, your mental skills. Affective domain, although important is often intentionally overlooked. It is the attitude, motivation and willingness to learn or participate. In short, your feelings and emotions. Lastly psychomotor relates to your physical/kinesthetic motor skills. This is your physical ability including but not limited to your vision, auditory and verbal imitations or the lack thereof. Why are these learning classifications referred to as domains, one might ask? Because they govern, rule or control the way things are conducted. Even though this is not a geographical location, it is still a specific arena. With every domain, there is some entity trying to exercise their power over it.

Blessed With Less

There are both natural and manmade or manipulated, inanimate powers that we are familiar with. Most of them we cannot govern or totally control. However, if released in full strength, unshaded would destroy most life forms. These powers are sources of energy, that we have learned how to harness, Channel, and in a limited manner contain. The most common are as follows: solar, wind, water, fire, steam, chemical, nuclear, internal combustion, animal and man power.

Solar power is the conversion of energy from sunlight into electricity. We cannot dictate when the sun appears or rotates; we cannot touch it, put it out nor claim ownership of it. We have been able to obtain an estimated distance of ninety-three million miles from the Earth. We were also able to estimate the constant, unwavering surface temperature of eleven thousand degrees Fahrenheit. However, this is still speculative since nothing can get close enough to the actual surface. None the less, we are now able to redirect and stabalize small portions of its rays to be used as a power source. Even at that distance the sun has produced a recorded heat on this earth of one hundred, thirty-six (136) degrees. The average human being uncovered and without hydration, exposed to that level of heat, would die in two (2) days.

Wind power, is the use of airflow through wind turbines to mechanically power generators for electric power. This is one of the cleaner forms of energy, very popular in the use of a windmill and on sail boats. Windmills are one of the first man-made methods of power generation. Modern terminology refers to windmills as turbines. Many are still in use today to pump water mostly on farms. They also used power generators that make electricity. They are mostly operated in open windy areas and when contained very useful. However, if presented in the form of a tornado, the only thing us humans can do is evacuate, or brace ourselves and pray we survive.

Water power also known as hydropower, is power derived from the energy produced from falling water or fast running water. Water power is one of the oldest known powers that was harnessed. Early civilization settled near water because of its life force. As the population grew they needed to get the water to the people. Devices for irrigation, ducts, cisterns and even toilets have been traced as far back as 2350 BC in Lothal India. As a power source evidence of a water driven wheel is found in the 3rd century BC in Perachora Greece. Water is necessary to hydrate Humans, animals and plant life. It is needful for cleanliness. However, in the form of a hurricane or a monsoon, mankind is outmatched.

The discovery of fire, is attributed to the extinct homo erectus population formerly known as Pithecanthropus erectus, having upright stature. Scientist date this back to 1.9 million years ago. Artifacts from South Africa's Wonderwerk Cave show evidence of charred animal bones and ashes plant remains. Excavation of that location began in 2004 and is still ongoing; per a paper written by lead author, Francesco Berna, a Boston University professor of archeology. It is noted that fire was also used to purify, more importantly it was a symbol of power. This harnessed energy was a force to be reckoned with and in many cultures worshipped. Several mythical names derived from fire; some we are familiar with are: Agni, the Hindu god of fire; Maman Brigitte, Afro-American mythological god. Ra, Sekhmet and Wadjet all Egyptian gods of fire, sun and warmth. The list is extensive, but most refers to the power of the sun and volcanoes. Those who learn to rub sticks together, spark rocks or Sulphur were feared and some even worshipped as gods. Eventually firearms were created, which was an actual weapon such as a gun or cannon. However it also denoted the amount of power one had, like the size of the military. Howbeit fire, although good for light warmth, purification and cooking is also a very dangerous source if not contained. Entire civilizations have been destroyed by natural fire. In 1906 an earthquake caused fires which destroyed 80% of San Francisco, CA here in the United States of America.

Steam power is derived from boiling water. The force of energy produced in that form has been used for over 2000 years, but wasn't practical until the year 1712 when the steam engine was developed. They were large and expensive to build. Steam power didn't replace water power but was used in conjunction. Stationary steam engines were used to power mills on farms. In the 1800's this technology was modified and was adopted all over the U.S.A. as an accepted alternative energy source. Some of the biggest developments were steam boats and the steam powered locomotive. By the middle of the nineteenth century virtually every American city contained shops producing steam engines. These engines revolutionized the industry in that they were being used to manufacture other machines. The hazards associated were steam burns, as well as those acquired from contact with that hot metal, but the most severe were those affected by explosions.

Chemical power is, energy created by a reaction which is stored in the bonds of chemical compounds (atoms and molecules). Often it produces heat as a by-product. Batteries, biomass, petroleum, natural gas and coal are all examples of stored chemical energy we use to power things. Although commonly used these chemicals have a tendency to leak causing severe burns and depending on what it is contained in, explosions.

Nuclear power is the use of nuclear reactions that release nuclear energy to generate heat which is frequently used in steam turbines to produce electricity. It is used all over the world logically because it produces energy that produces other forms of energy at an accelerated rate. It is also one of the most environmentally friendly sources of energy, especially when compared to a coal burning power plant. However, the downside is if there is an accident or even a leak, large quantities of radioactive material could be released into the environment. Nuclear waste remains radioactive and is hazardous to health for thousands of years.

Internal combustion is an engine such as an automotive gasoline engine in which fuel is burned within the engine as opposed to an external one like on a steam engine. The first person known to have experimented with an internal-combustion engine was the Dutch physicist Christian Huygens in 1680. But no effective gasoline powered engine was developed until 1859, almost two hundred years later. Today in every country you can find a gasoline powered automobile or even an airplane which uses an internal-combustible engine. It's clearly convenient, very powerful and cost effective. However, the flip side is it produces a large amount of pollution, high maintenance, and a very limited lifetime. It also could ignite flammable gases or vapors, which is dangerous, and the consequences could be potentially devastating.

Animal power is that which uses the energy of animals to power or move objects. They were once used to plow fields, pull carriages and sleds, that function has mostly been replaced by machines. Except in regions with rough terrain, or wooded areas Animal power is pretty much limited to leisure rides. Animals in general don't maintain a long productive life. But they have been noted as good loyal companions. However, in recent years there has been an up rise of animal attacks on humans. There is a categorized list of twenty-five animal species responsible for the death of humans. The tiny mosquito is regarded as the most deadly; killing an estimated three million people per year.

Man-power is the physical labor of mankind. It was once one of the most cost-effective forms of power especially if they were enslaved. Man-power is also measured by the amount of people involved as opposed to just one's individual strength. It is believed that machines will never be able to totally replace manpower. For every machine and or artificial intelligence, a human is still needed to program, monitor and maintain it. In today's time man-power is used in the multi-billion-dollar prison industrial system, in the same manner as slavery was; obtaining free or very cheap labor. In a twisted way, it is still productive, although job descriptions may have changed. Mankind, is still the most disruptive, destructive, and dangerous of them all.

In the beginning, God created heaven and earth. The 1st chapter of Genesis states, God created man and woman; placed them in the garden and gave them dominion over everything. Along with dominion, they inherently had power and authority. Sometimes when we have everything, our feelings get the best of us. We must be ever so careful to guard whatever we have. No matter how we obtained it, if we are not careful we can lose it. That is the case with these two, they didn't guard what was entrusted to them, subsequently they were put out of said garden. How can one have dominion without a domain? How do you lose something so great? Any time you use anything outside of its prescribed manner that is called abuse. Some have a sense of entitlement, others neglect. At some point, they were operating in the conflicting state of cognitive dissonance. They got torn between two thoughts and ultimately operated in their own power.

We need to recognize that all power comes from and belongs to God. The sooner we realize this the closer we are to understanding that everything we have regarding power, authority and or dominion, is created, delegated and regulated by God. We will then wisely submit ourselves to the higher power and position ourselves to be blessed.

Chapter 7

Less,
Lack,
Mediocrity

Have you ever been made to feel inadequate, insignificant or just plain "less than"; whether intentionally or unintentionally? Whether it was because of your physical stature, your financial portfolio, your education, the location of your residence, your social or political status. How about, not really knowing when it was happening, then finding out days, months or even years later that someone viewed or referenced you in a trivialized or demeaning manner? I'm going to mention a few things, some about myself and some about others which I have encountered on this journey. Both I'm sure you will be able to understand, relate to, and maybe even personally identify with. Hopefully you weren't the one causing another to feel like they were less.

In the home of my parents I was the one who was perceived as, deemed, labeled and doomed to have less. I was the youngest of seven, the skinniest, and the least educated, to this day. My siblings had academic GPA's to be proud of, as opposed to my let's just leave it at barely passing; although the politically correct term I believe would probably be "socially promoted". Their stats in the athletic field were publicized as phenomenal; although I made the teams and had playing time. I was actually very good, but they were great, and their greatness outshined my goodness every day. I, from a stand still position, could physically jump clear over the front end of a full-size car; and could run a mile in four (4) minutes and twenty (20) seconds flat, but I was still called "Little Rabbit". Normally that name in and of itself would be fine until you take note that I wasn't called little because of my height, weight or even age, but because my brother was the original Rabbit and he could jump higher, further and could run faster. They never had to call him big rabbit, just simply rabbit. Ironically in the line of succession he was outshined by the brother older than him. This brother was the most logical, so he acquired the title and name Mr. Spock". Yes, a direct correlation and comparison to the fictional "Vulcan" character in the "Star Trek media franchise". To no surprise, that brother had to concede to the oldest brother who was known all over as "Doctor Vee", even though he held no official documented medical or Doctorate degree. He was a reader extraordinaire, and wasn't limited to any one specific specialty but was well versed in many subjects and could retain and recall large volumes of information. He maintained a 3.9 GPA through every level of education. Although Dr. Vee was the oldest male he was still subject to my oldest sister who held the grandest of professional titles.

They all went into professional, favorable, desirable and conversation worthy careers; they dealt with paper and the development of people whereas I dealt with prisoners. Growing up we were taught to seek out the preferred prestigious careers; they were: Doctor, Lawyer, Professor/Teacher, Firefighter and Police. No one ever glorified being a Sanitation worker or Correction Officer. As fore stated I fell in the lot of the latter, NYDOC. My siblings had new cars and houses, I had an apartment and a used car. Their friends, colleagues and even casual associates referred to me as the little one. If anyone has ever watched the Chris Rock show, "Everybody hates Chris" let's just say I never got the big piece of chicken.

In similitude, several of my friends had mothers who constantly reminded them how much less of a man their father was. Some because they were physically small, some in stature, some in height or weight. Some were called less than because of their educational level while others because of their financial condition. The dads that were most notably, negatively impacted, degraded and or denounced were those who were still present. Moreover, some dads weren't just present, but were active and productive, however, were not given the respect or recognition. My Dad did not have a grand formal education, but he did not lack in intelligence. He could do, and or fix almost anything. He was one of the strongest men I ever knew. But because of the social climate we lived in, he was still referred to as mediocre by our society. My mother passed when I was 16, I had less time with her than my siblings but no lack. She was a pro by the time she got to me. I got the express fully developed and cultivated parental training.

For many this next series of my personal recollection is just old news. For those that are tired of hearing about racism, inequality and the woes of the down trodden; imagine how tired those of us who are experiencing what you are merely repeatedly hearing about feel. I would love to let bygones be bygones. I wish I could just forget about some of the issues of the so called past; but someone, somewhere, somehow keeps reminding me. It would be a little easier to forgive and forget that past if it weren't still currently our present.

I attended Canarsie High school in Brooklyn, NY. Prior to me attending I physically marched with my mother in order for my older brothers to attend. The racial climate previously prevented people of color from attending that school. Even once people of color were allowed in, we were constantly reminded of our "place". I had one of the few homes that actually had two parents cohabitating. Not only did I have two parents but they both had full time jobs. They taught us that we had to do everything with excellence. Albeit we being "non-white" had to be at least twice as good as our counterparts, to be accepted, although still not equal. You had to be wise and not flaunt your ability; but remain humble giving credit and accolades to our counterparts.

The structured social powers of Canarsie were divided between the Italian and Jewish communities. We the people of color were never considered equal, but we consistently strived to achieve the prestigious label of less than. I looked into the constitution of the United States of America and discovered that I as well as every black person was still listed as 3/5 of a human. How much less can you get than to be labeled by default before you were even born. For more than half of the 19th century we the (black) people didn't have a right to vote, and even longer if you were female. To this day there is still no place where complete equal opportunity is practiced. Those in power somehow always find a way to discriminate. Their general premise is that the individual, class or group is not on an equal level as them. Dare I say they believe they are superior and that everyone else is inferior or "less than".

In corporate America two individuals may be the same age, gender, height and weight; and also have the same education, and experience, but if they have a different race somehow, they will be viewed differently. And the general response is: the one with the lighter skin had that something special, that extra something, that something more. If by chance, there were two positions to be filled, the previous one would somehow have more benefits and or a higher rate of pay. On one of my previous jobs, I made over a million dollars for the company in one single year. My Christmas bonus was $150. My successor who I was training the following Christmas received two weeks in Vienna Austria, a house and a company car; as a bonus. Thus, showing clear disparity simultaneously awarding one with more and inherently depriving the other with less.

I remember hearing corporations using the infamous unwritten slogan of "doing more with less". I immediately thought they were talking about me, thinking finally I was about to be put in a position, to do more; that's how much I associated myself with "Less". The promulgation of this mindset is as strong now as it ever was. Some innuendos are subtle, vague and even cloaked; while others are bold and blatant. One former Congressman John Andrew Boehner will go down in history as one who single handedly, opposed, withstood, and probably, imposed more congressional strangle holds on a sitting U.S. President in history thus far. This then

Chapter 7 Less, Lack, Mediocrity

Republican, Speaker of the House of Representatives, was being forced to resign from that position. As he mounted the podium preceding his resignation speech, in September 2015, he in an entitled posture and in clear defiance, arrogantly, publicly, sang the following lyrics:

> *"Zip-A-Dee-Doo-Dah*
> *Zip-A-Dee-A*
> *My oh my what a wonderful day*
> *Plenty of sunshine headed my way*
> *"Zip-A-Dee-Doo-Dah*
> *Zip-A-Dee-A*

This song ultimately ends with the phrase:

> *"Everything's going my way".*

This is a song from the 1946 academy award winning Disney film "Song of the South" which I was previously fond of, until I grew up and saw how this show projected and programed mentalities that one should be happy in a degraded state. Disney has not acknowledged the racism associated with this semi-animated film, but it has been removed from public view since the mid 1980's. that removal in an of itself is a strong indicator of how insulting it was. In same respect it shows the power and superiority which allowed Disney to just remove it without having to compensate anyone for the harm it caused.

Logically and historically the eldest had rule. Dare I say at every level, whether it was middle school, high school or college, there was always at least one, but the general

Blessed With Less

consensus, is that someone was always superior, and you were always "less than". Do you remember your freshman year of any school you attended? Traditionally the sophomores picked on the freshman, the juniors picked on the sophomores, and the seniors picked on the juniors. If you pledged in a sorority, you were simply that; a pledge. You were there to be the butt of jokes, to be: hazed, humiliated, used and abused. If you played on a team, you were the rookie, bench warmer, towel boy, water boy, ball boy, bat boy and any other demeaning belittling "boy". This cycle continued into the work force. The newest employees had to take all the flak from not only boss(s) but also tenured employees.

In the work force, you were called green or nothing more than "the new guy". That meant you were the "gopher", go for this, go for that. You ran errands, made and served coffee, many times at your expense. If you were invited to a social event, it was so you could pick up the tab. You were the lackey, flunky, do whatever I say guy / girl. A mere minion in this despicable world. When I first entered the New York City Department of Correction as a new employee, we were called "new jacks". We were on probation and could be fired for "cause". You got it, any cause they felt like utilizing. We had little to no rights, we paid union dues but were told by the union that there was little the union could do to secure our job. We were told to figuratively walk on egg shells and cater to the bosses and senior officers, at least until after probation. While gaining this wonderful experience, I noticed the inmates held to the same structure. You heard terms like: fresh meat, fish on the line, Vic (as in victim) and jail bait if they were young.

Chapter 7 Less, Lack, Mediocrity

Finally, you matriculate, you have tenure, you even have a title, but the reality now shows its self. Some owner of the company or their spoiled kid has to show you that they're greater, richer, more important and ultimately, that you work for them and that they own you.

Unless you had the priviledge of some favorable nepotism the newest, youngest and or poorest were of less importance, the least of anyone's concerns. The good news is knowing that less is different than lack. Speaking optimistically the less responsibility means a lighter work load. You may think your work load is a lot, however the weight of vicarious liability on the person(s) responsible are enormous. If anyone has had the task of changing your residence, at some point do you not wish that you had less furniture and clothes to move? If you ever have taken a trip with or without additional baggage fees, do you sometimes wish you had less to carry. If you do physical exercise, especially if you swim is it wise to do it with a full stomach or do you wish you had eaten less. Do you prefer to exercise or swim fully clothed, wearing a hat coat and shoes. I know that seems ridiculous but that is often the downside of having more.

It is truly amazing how truth can be twisted, manipulated and or taken out of context. One of the most common lessons taught was, how it was an honor to be modest, humble and ready to give, more than to receive. Catholic Priests actually take a vow of poverty. But I took note that Less did not equate with nor constitute lack. Not many could casually refer to an individual with that level of dedication and consistency as mediocre. I temporarily

Blessed With Less

gained some solace in seeing several portions of scripture. Although somewhat fragmented, Mathew 5:3-12 quotes Jesus as saying: "Blessed are the poor", "Blessed are they that mourn", "Blessed are they that do hunger and thirst", "Blessed are they which are persecuted". This is referred to as alternative truths, wherein part of the truth is revealed to shape ones' opinion. My perception of the scriptures in its entirety was distorted. Even down to the little bit of knowledge of the biblical principal of sowing and reaping. Talk about getting it all wrong, I ultimately subscribed to the notion that I was supposed to always have less. My lack caused me to doubt so much that I thought I couldn't afford to sow. Think of the confusion of believing but not really trusting, both without understanding. I later came to realize that "the poor" referenced wasn't monetary, and it ends with theirs is the kingdom of heaven and money cannot get you there. Furthermore "mourning" was having compassion, your reward is, you also will be comforted. Moreover, hunger and thirst was not for physical natural food, but for righteousness; the bottom line result, is you will be filled. And finally, persecuted was only beneficial if it was for "His" sake. Unfortunately, if you are persecuted for your own wrong doing, that's called justice. Sometime God will extend mercy and you don't get the full justice deserved.

In my misinformed uneducated state, I would have argued that anyone who subscribed to the "more is less" philosophy was an under achiever. As usual some subjective individual challenged my use of the term "more is less" because they were only familiar with the opposite point of view which is "less is more". Initially I couldn't quite pinpoint where I saw the concept and I had too many

85

years of mis-catalogued research and so little time. That bit of information just reminded me that too many words can many times obscure the point. I recently came across a book entitled minimalism: Live with a meaningful life. In this journey co-authors Joshua Fields Millburn & Ryan Nicodemus explore opposite perspectives. They presented the argument: "Having more time causes less frustration and less stress, more freedom adds less anxiety and less worry. But more meaning in our lives allows us to focus far less on life's excess in favor of what's truly important." In contrast, they continue by saying, "Owning less stuff, focusing on fewer tasks, and having less in the way has given us more time, more freedom, and more meaning in our lives. Working less allows us to contribute more, grow more, and pursue our passions much more." Their conclusion; "So, more is less? Yes, more or less."

I saw a movie years ago, entitled: "The Fly". In this film, the main character was a scientist. He was so engulfed in his work that he sought ways to limit distractions. One that initially struck me as odd, but I later learned to appreciate was his wardrobe selection. He purchased multiple pieces of the exact same outfit, in its entirety; same color, pattern and size. To an outsider, it would appear as though this scientist was wearing the same clothes every day. Technically he was, but with the liberty of having a clean set to put on and simultaneously allowing him the freedom of one less decision to make daily. The same concept is practiced in many organizations today. School and work environment utilize uniforms to create a level of unity and equality. However, it also accomplishes the same goal of having less to think about, thus giving more time and

Blessed With Less

attention to getting dressed in a timely fashion and also more time to concentrate on the specified tasks relative to that environment. These practices many would argue shows how to work smarter as opposed to harder. However, there is a distinct difference between working smarter which is doing less work while effectively getting the job done. As opposed to being lazy, which will most likely end in a mediocre job performance at the least. In the worst scenario, the lack will be clear and evident and probably result in failure.

Bill Cosby is an American musician, author activist, actor, comedian, education and television producer. His net worth is four hundred million dollars. Through scandals, accusations and alleged lack of integrity and morals, he is now publicly viewed as "less than". He has more than fifty accusers. If found guilty, and was ordered to compensate his victims, anywhere between five and fifty million dollars each, plus legal fees, he potentially could lose his entire fortune. He would no longer just have a feeling of less, but it would be actual and may even become lack. Oprah Winfrey is the second richest African American in the U.S.A. but she has less money than President Donald Trump. Both Michael Bloomberg and Warren Buffet each have ten times as much money as Donald Trump. All of these Billionaires have less money than Bill Gates, but none of them are lacking. Neither did they obtain their wealth with a mediocre work ethic, although some have capitalized through unethical tactics. If we had less indiscretions and would maximize our work ethic, without selfishly trying to please ourselves we would have no lack. More importantly, we would then be in a more favorable position with God and that is being blessed.

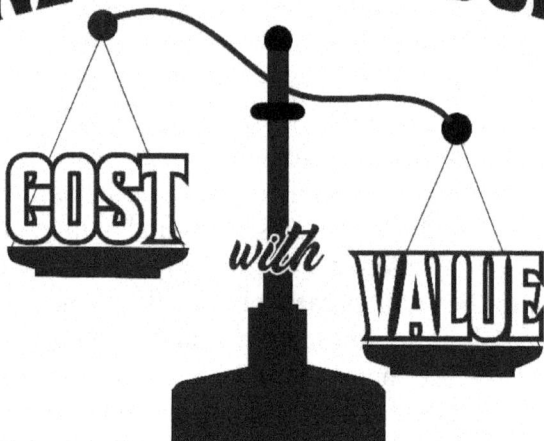

NEVER CONFUSE COST *with* VALUE

SALVATION IS FREE
ISIAH 55:1

Chapter 8

Position,
Timing,
Qualification

There is a great feeling of optimism, regardless of your personal qualifications, when we are in "the right place at the right time". As opposed to the defeated feeling that is associated with being in the wrong place at the wrong time. But when is the right or wrong time, and how is that determined? With the first position, you don't necessarily have to be the most qualified, you just must be available; hence that would be considered, in the right place. However, with the second position there is less room for minimal qualification or skill. When you are in a deviated position, your skill level must over compensate.

The term position, has ambiguous meanings. I have chosen two major types of positions, that I've summed up as, geographical and non-geographical. However, there are also multiple subdivisions within those two types. Those position variations, also referred to as postures, are as follows: physical, mental, emotional, and spiritual. In real estate, there is a popular, phrase used when promoting an expensive property; "Location, location, location". Sometimes the property itself isn't that spectacular, however the location may be prime. That structure may be small and even dilapidated, but if it's positioned right, if it's in the right

city, on the right street, near the right attraction, and or in the right market, its value increases drastically. By the same standards, you may find a huge, immaculate building, but it's in a flood zone, or an area prone to tornadoes, hurricanes, earthquakes or crime; that property value will be less. Moreover, there may not be any imminent danger of disaster but, if the location is less popular or that economy is struggling, you now have a depreciated property. Maybe you are not into real estate and can't appreciate the previous analogy. Imagine have all your favorite foods and desserts, prepared for you and your guests. Now picture it being served on trashcan lids. On a historical note, Lot, the nephew of the great patriarch Abraham, move to a city called Sodom. Although he had much, he chose to separate from his blessed uncle because, his herdsmen couldn't get along with his uncle's herdsmen. He was in the wrong place, at the wrong time. His state of mind is debatable, but he had to be ushered out of the city before God destroyed it.

Staying in the geographical vain, there is a location within a location, which denotes how things are arranged within a specific location. If we stay with the example of real estate; we need to consider, how the inside is structured, for it affects the value. The aesthetics, or how it is decorated can affect the visual appeal. Not many people can see past the exterior structure and continue to look for the value inside. So now we have established that we may have a very nice structure, in a very nice location. Now consider the exterior needing a cosmetic makeover. Let's further picture everything inside out of place, or position. The oven is in the bedroom, the refrigerator is in the bathroom and the sink is in the closet. Sounds ridiculous but clearly gives us a horrendous visual of a position within a position. In an analogy of spheres, I've discovered that the Biosphere, which is man, was made from the Geosphere which is earth. That same earth was used to separate the Hydrosphere, which surrounded by the Atmosphere which is air. Globally this does not change, man is in the earth, earth is in the water, and water is in the air.

When reciting the "Our Fathers" prayer which Jesus taught to his disciples (Matthew 6:9-13), do we really consider what we're saying? It was designed for us to incorporate a new manner of conducting ourselves. We are asking that God's will be done in the earth as it is in heaven. That earth is ambiguously referring to the general earth we live in and the specific inner man being biproducts of the earth. But, in order for that to take place, we must do as the prayer instructed us, which is to desire and strive that our will conform and become His will. When this happens, we will then see and ask for things that are in line with what He would want. In short, the Apostle Paul writes this admonishment; "Let this mind be in you which was also in Christ Jesus" (Philippians 2:5). For some this is extreme, but for those who have children, when they ask for money or a gift, is it not easier to give when they are asking for something you approve of? Does it not make it hard to say no if they've done all their chores and homework; finally present their request with a humble smile? The posture they present puts them in a much better position for you to bless them, how much more should the God expect form us. On the other hand, let that same child show up, with an attitude that's not so humble; missing homework, chores incomplete, requesting anything, you might subject them to the food the least like. You won't let them starve, but they kind of put you in a position, where you have to remind them as the old folks would say, what side their bread was buttered on. They were so close, but their position changed yours.

Have you ever had a near miss? Have you ever been so geographically close that you've had the occasion to utilize the phrase "another coat of paint and we would have had an accident"? Have you ever accidentally cut yourself, gone to the doctor and they tell you "a little further over, or a little deeper" and the result could have been more severely catastrophic or even fatal. Have you ever missed your ride, be it a bus, train, ship or plane, and you were so close that you were able to see it leaving? Or you hear later that the vessel that you would've been on was involved in an accident? This list of incidents which we were spared from could be quite lengthy, if we examine all the unintended positions we have been in. On the flip side, there were also several opportunities, both missed, and obtained by being in some of those same positions. Let's say you are in a vehicle; you have the right of way, and you are hit by another vehicle. You were in the right place, but accidents happen, however, you were fortunately wearing your seatbelt, which allowed you to reduce your injuries. The slightest variation in position could have drastically changed the outcome.

Have you ever played, or even watched any sporting event, whether it was an individual or team competition? In any fighting sport, boxing, wrestling, or martial arts, one of the first set of instructions given includes this seemingly obvious phrase, "protect yourself at all times". Often a punch or kick is thrown before or after the bell. The bewildered recipient of that strike may get seriously hurt and or knocked out, because they weren't in a position to defend themselves. There is a term known as "off sides", it is used in football, hockey and soccer. In all three sports, it involves players being out of a legal position with regard to the specific rules of that game. In basketball, there are so many ways to be out of position. If you step on the court before being acknowledged by the officials. Or if during a foul shot you cross the three second zone before the shooter releases the ball. You are in violation and with each of those, and you haven't even touched the ball. If you then continue by stepping out of bounds, or basket interference, also known as goal tending, which is touching the ball as it is coming down over the basket. A good game is usually noted when teams are strategically executing both offensive and defensive tactics. Most significant plays involve the position the players are in. With basketball, they used a term called boxing out. It was primarily for rebounding purposes. The premise was no matter how athletic your opponent was, if you boxed him out of position, it would increase your probability of obtaining that rebound. Whoever sets the best picks, an offensive blocking technic usually affording an accompanying player a clearer shot. In baseball, the ball must stay within the noted boundaries, or it is labeled a foul ball, which is out of play position.

There is also a term known as "caught napping". This term is used when a defensive field player sneaks up behind an offensive runner and tags him out. This is only possible when said runner is not on base which is "out of position". In addition to not being on base that same runner is not paying attention to the actions of the defending players on the field. In their defense, being out of position as a runner is legal as long as you don't get tagged out. In almost every sport when someone says, "you got beat" although the game has not yet ended; they are inferring that you got beat to the better position.

If you hunt animals, there is a time of day conducive to hunting specific animals. There is also a strategic location to place yourself in for the best results, as well as a proper way to hold and use your weapon. You should be close enough to see your target, yet far enough to be undetected and safe. Based on your qualifications and level of expertise, you may need to be closer in order to effectively reach your target. You must be able to gauge to speed of a moving animal, aiming for the place you anticipate it going as opposed to where it currently is.

As a part of any corporation, team or organization, everyone has a specific position. Every job site has a restricted, or limited access area. Your Position, title and or security clearance determines how much access you have. There are Managers, Supervisors and subordinates. Within those positions are those with seniority and those with a special skill set. Few have all access, a private office and or restroom, and maybe even a reserved parking space. Some, have authority to view some files but cannot make changes. In general, if everyone plays their position, stays in their lane, and does their job, the end result will be successful. However, what happens when we are out of position? Most fall out of position simply because they refuse to follow orders, rules and regulations. That oxymoronic deliberate refusal to act, is actually an action called insubordination. When anything, especially people, are out of position nothing functions correctly. If managers are not managing, supervisors are not supervising and subordinates are insubordinate, not only are you subject to malfunction you are at risk of total chaos. It would be like trying to drive a car while in park or neutral. You will be in the car coasting, drifting or sitting still, none of which qualifies as driving. You can sleep in the wrong position and wake up sore. You can lift an object in the wrong position and cause injury to yourself.

Have you ever endeavored to obtain a home? You went searching and found your dream home. It was the right size, in the right neighborhood. You then went to the real estate broker who in turn brought you to the mortgage banker. The banker loved your presentation and personality, and thought you were going to be a great candidate to do business with. However, that is when you receive a very clear assessment of your true financial position. They noted that you had a good job with a good income, but your debt ratio was not acceptable. You were not in a good enough financial position to secure a loan from them. You were also that same week, informed by your landlord that they will not be renewing your lease. What a precarious position to be in.

You have finally comfortably positioned yourself, in an attempt, to go to sleep, but it is now time to go to work. You have already received a final warning from your job, due to your repeated lateness. You have finally positioned yourself with the political candidate of your choice, but the election has already ended. You finally decide to take your relationship seriously, but your significant other has already made other plans. The day you get up to pay your overdue car note, you find your vehicle has already been towed. Does any of this sound familiar? A day late and a dollar short. Many have said, timing is everything. Have you ever seen a good athlete, but his rhythm was off, and he just couldn't get his timing together? He may have been in great physical shape, and put forth a valiant effort, but without all three components operating together, at the same time, he may come close but will not win. Hence, we have opportunity to use the not so glorious phrase; "so close, yet so far".

Furthermore, there is another variation of position; that which is relative of posture. While posture can be physical, it can also be mental, emotional and or spiritual. It can be unintentional, such as indecisiveness, where one fails to act. However, it is mostly intentional; when one takes this type of position, they willfully agree to oppose something or someone, even if only in a passive aggressive manner. Imagine an officer of the law idly watching a crime in progress and choosing not to respond. In contrast, another officer is undercover, or in a position where the assailant has the advantage, although qualified, that may be the best time to remain quiet. When you cast a vote, it is usually because of your position or view of the subject being voted on. The paralysis of analysis, is one pondering on the position they should take. including how one should present themselves, do I conform to the dress code, conduct code, language code, all these are positions we face throughout our lives. My parents taught all of us (their children), proper etiquette. How to stand erect, how to sit, and how to walk. How to set a table, including how to hold all of the utensils. We were taught how to present ourselves when in public. When to speak, when to look a person in the eye, and when you should avoid eye contact. For those of us who remember the Emmet Till story, his confrontation began with him not understanding the rules of the south. Specific rules like walking in the street or on the other side of the street, when passing white people. Not looking them in the eye, but looking down in a passive submissive manner. Speaking only when spoken to and only on the subject they introduce, not your ideas or philosophy. Had he understood that posture, there never would have come an occasion to make any comment, sound or gesture that even appeared to be an advance or form of disrespect. Do you know your place? Be it in society, at work, in your home and or with God?

Here is the pacifying solace with which we comfort, or should I say, delude ourselves. We know we have such great qualities and potential, and we also believe that there will be plenty of other opportunities for us to take advantage of. We count our certifications and degrees. We revel in our perception of how great we are. We reflect on our accomplishments, while building our emotional and psychological memorials of our past achievements. We have now become victims of delusions of grandeur. The fact is, our qualifications are subjective. We may have a degree and even experience in a specific subject, but what qualifies us is our position. You may be a great candidate for a particular office but your position with regard to that arena may disqualify you. For beauty is in the eyes of the beholder. The question is whose approval and or what position are you seeking? The physical position may be advantageous, you may have the natural qualifications, but is it your time? And is that time in conjunction with God's will?

In the book of 1st Samuel, the eighth chapter, we see the beginning of a story which details an individual with qualities, but who was later disqualified. When Israel pleaded for a king, they got exactly what they asked for. When choosing him, the unanimous consensus was that "he looked the part". He was a Benjamite, a mighty man of power, and taller than most. It is even said that he was a goodly man. That man's name was Saul, and at the request of the people, he became the 1st king of Israel. The prophet Samuel tried to discourage the people saying, God was their king, but they petitioned the more saying: they wanted one they could see. "And the Lord said unto Samuel, Hearken unto the voice of the people in all that they say unto thee: for they have not rejected thee, but they have rejected me, that I should not reign over them". Prior to this appointment, God revealed to, and instructed Samuel to protest and inform the people what manner of king he would be. Samuel continued with a brief description saying: "He will take your sons, and appoint them for himself". "And he will take your daughters to be confectionaries, and to be cooks, and to be bakers". "He will take your fields, and your vineyards, and your oliveyards, even the best of them, and give them to his servants". In his final plea he said: "And ye shall cry out in that day because of your king which ye shall have chosen you; and the Lord will not hear you in that day". "Nevertheless, the people refused to obey the voice of Samuel; and they said, Nay; but we will have a king over us". "That we also may be like all the nations; and that our king may judge us, and go before us, and fight our battles". After Samuel heard the words of the people, the Lord said unto him, "hearken unto their voice, and make them a king".

God extended opportunity to the people to show their position, or posture towards Him. Their outspoken position caused them to be unqualified to be His people at that current time. He then conceded to allow another individual to be the king they asked for. Amazingly they voluntarily chose to forfeit the place(position) they had with God. Can you imagine trading a spirit and all-powerful being, for a mere mortal, who was self-serving and didn't have the best interest of the people, or God's will in mind. How could an individual with this mindset lead and or judge the people of God? With all his height, strength and goodly ways; with what power would he lead the people into battle? Especially since Israel wasn't a nation of warriors, they needed the protection and guidance of the Lord. For it is "Not by might, nor by power, but by my spirit, saith the Lord of hosts". When we look at how their biggest battles were won; we find it wasn't with carnal weapons, but with prayer, fasting and praise. Saul's successor David was anointed king and went back to tending sheep, not because he wasn't qualified, nor because he was shirking his call, but because it wasn't time. There he maintained his position, awaiting his appropriate authorized time.

Throughout history we see a plethora of examples of people who either had the wrong posture, had terrible timing and or lacked qualifications. Adam and Eve were the first; notice their posture after they disobeyed; they hid themselves. Knowing they were naked, which meant exposed. They were no longer in a "right position" with God. Then following in the same path, their son Cain displayed a questionable posture after killing his brother. In his unqualified state, he still attempted to present to God. The ten spies who held a different position from Joshua and Caleb. It is no coincidence that only Joshua and Caleb made it to the promised land. Those ten spies and all the other adults complained and murmured; end result God killed them. Consider your current daily life, have you ever noticed the posture of someone who doesn't quite fit in a particular environment? Usually their intentions are not good and make them obviously suspicious. When you consider the event, you often wonder, was it happenstance that they showed up on this day at this time. Sometimes they are the victim, but their posture tells you something is wrong. Think of an abused individual or even an animal and their posture when an abuser is present. There is a clear visibly physical posture showing fear, confidence, submission and arrogance. For those with any level of discernment those same postures can be recognized and identified spiritually. If these postures can be seen and either appreciated or abhorred by mere mortal men, how much more do you believe God sees and expects. Have you considered your position recently?

Where you place yourself geographically does not necessarily dictate or regulate who you are, but it is relative. It cannot alone dictate our destiny, but can affect how we grow. It can affect how much harder it will be and how much more assistance we will need to accomplish the same task, if performed in a more conducive environment might be effortless. "There went out a sower to sow, and it came to pass, as he sowed, some fell by the way" (Mark 4:3-4). It continues saying, some fell on stony ground, some fell among thorns and other fell on good ground. Three out of the four grew into something but only for a short period of time. Although not written in the scripture, horticulture notes that many seeds are replanted by the animals that consume them. In the fourth verse of Mark 4, it states that the fowls of the air came and devoured that which was sown by the wayside. It is reasonable to believe those seeds grew elsewhere. Only that which was sown on good ground, is noted as yielding, up to an hundred fold. Abraham's Nephew Lot, a very conflicting character, chose to go to Sodom. His mentality(posture) caused him to move out of the position he was in. his sight told him that the land looked good and bountiful, therefore he should move. We have to very mindful of the fact that we although are grown enough to make decisions, does not mean we shouldn't seek counsel with regard to the decisions we make. You will note at a certain point and time that proved to be the wrong destination. Has your mindset taken you to a place you ordinarily would not have gone?

Finally, there are also two major aspects of time I would like to address. Kairos (καιρός) is an ancient Greek word meaning the right or opportune moment (the supreme moment). God's time is always the right time and is always now. He is eternal, and is not just in, but He is the past, present and future, simultaneously. The ancient Greeks had two words for time, chronos and kairos. While the former refers to chronological or sequential time, the latter signifies a time lapse, a moment of indeterminate time in which everything happens. In brief, chronos, is chronological, where we count seconds, minutes, hours, days, months, years, periods and centuries. God created time for us. Kairos is Gods (now) time. We must stay tuned to His instructions so we can be where we need to be, when we need to be there. Anytime the posture of any individual isn't in alignment with God's will, they expose their position, display their lack of qualification, and the time for them is over.

They say,

"NO MAN IS AN ISLAND"

However, I say,

"ANYONE WHO THINKS THEY'RE AN ISLAND SHOULD PREPARE TO SOON BE DESERTED"

The ≠ Poet Joel

Chapter 9

Greedy,
Selfish,
Spiteful

One of the most commonly known seven deadly sins is greed. Wanting a lot is not necessarily greedy however there is a thin line. Some are extremely ambitious, some have a gifted savvy business sense, and inherently acquire a lot of substance. Some actually profess to need more than others to accomplish the same tasks. So, what is it that really constitutes greed? Most people who are greedy are also selfish. Valuing and or protecting your possessions in and of itself, doesn't make one selfish. But when you become spiteful to a point where you would rather destroy something rather than see someone else with it; well that is a clearer indicator of one, if not all of the aforementioned issues.

There was an occasion recorded in 1st Kings the third chapter, where one of the wisest men ever, king Solomon had to judge a dispute between two women. Both women were harlots, dwelling in the same house and both had recently given birth. One of the women, on one dismal night, accidently laid on and smothered her child while sleeping. When she realized that her child was dead she stole the other women's baby. Switching her dead son with the other woman's, claiming the live child belonged to her, and the dead child was the other woman's. Solomon in his wisdom suggested they cut the child in half and divide him between the two women. The kidnapper agreed that it was a good solution, but the real mother said she would rather see her son alive and raised by a stranger then to be cut in half.

In this one scenario, we see all three issues exhibited. Greed will cause you to take even that which doesn't belong to you. Selfishness will cause you to take without concern for others. Spite will cause you to intentionally inflict another knowing the outcome could be devastating. Sometimes that devastation is also applied to one's own self; giving occasion to use the phrase "cut off your nose to spite your face". This familiar expression is used to describe a needlessly self-destructive over-reaction to a problem. This idiom references someone acting without thinking the whole thing through. Most of the time the reaction of that individual causes more trouble than original problem. With all the issues that were displayed, I paid attention, in particular to, the things that were not variables, used to make judgement. Solomon never addressed the financial, political, racial or even religious state of anyone involved. He objectively based his decision on the root issue, the living child and the true mother. Something to consider when we are faced with situations that warrant our discretion and decision.

Everyone pretty much knows someone who is greedy, but most of us won't admit to being greedy ourselves. Most people associate greedy with someone obese. Although relative, there is an extreme difference. Certainly, habitually eating more than you need is called gluttony, and the physical result in all probability will be obesity. I therefore will concede that many greedy people are also obese. However, there are other possible contributing factors to their girth; namely lack of exercise, genetics, sickness and medications. Nonetheless, a misnomer that must be dispelled, is simply put, all obese individuals are not greedy, neither are all greedy individuals obese. If obesity is not rock-solid proof of greed, how would one know; and again, I ask, what constitutes greed?

Greed is the strong desire for more than you need, or maybe even can use. Greed is not limited to food but is frequently exhibited in the craving for wealth or power. Often lust is labeled as greed, but that is not always the case. Although lust and greed both exhibit a strong desire and coveting, lust is normally attributed desire of another human being and generally in a sexual nature. However, it still does not necessarily make it greed. In the study, specifically of the root reason of sexual assaults, Wikipedia documents several possible debatable causes, which include: military conquest, psychopathy, socioeconomics, ethical standards, attitudes towards victims, evolutionary pressures, sadism, laws, anger and power. Ironically none of the causes were attributed to greed. The psychological evaluations revealed that rape specifically, noted that the offender was obsessed with power. Especially with repeat offenders, you have the extreme case of someone whether with the same victim or several have done this same heinous crime multiple times. They may be classified as many different things, including selfish, but still may not be greedy.

"He that is greedy of gain troubleth his own house; but he that hateth gifts shall live". Proverbs 15:27. One of the many wise sayings of King Solomon, this one showing the association of greed with trouble. When one is greedy, they also become more gullible and or ruthless. Both are negative attributes which cause the individual to be lead about or driven, based on their insatiable longing. A greedy person can be bought, especially if they are passive. In contrast, an aggressive greedy individual becomes callous and sometimes brutal. Always wanting more, never having enough; resulting in unethical tactics such as extortion, stealing, kidnapping and even murder. Flamboyant millionaire Malcolm Forbes is most known for this, but it was Francine Morrissette who coined the phrase "He who dies with the most stuff wins". Having a lot of things is not a crime or a sin, however, what you do with that abundance will cause you to be judged accordingly. "For unto whomsoever much is given, of him shall be much required; and to whom men have committed much, of him they will ask the more" Luke 12:48. "And if a man strive for masteries, yet is he not crowned, except he strive lawfully" 2nd Timothy 2:5. These scriptures address how we obtain, and what we do with what we have, whether it is a little or an abundance.

In Acts the 5th chapter there is a recorded lesson of a married couple, Ananias and his wife Sapphira. They wanted to give the appearance that they were willing to give, just like everyone else had volunteered to do. Much to our disappointment, they conspired and lied about the amount they were giving. In their defense, the money was lawfully theirs to do with as they pleased. However, they made a pledge to the church, that they would sell a possession and all the proceeds would go to the church. Somewhere between greed and selfishness, they reneged. The Apostle Peter challenged the amount of gift and asked Ananias, "why hath Satan filled thine heart to lie to the Holy Ghost" Acts 5:3. He continued with a statement; "thou hast not lied unto men, but unto God. Acts 5:4. Immediately Ananias dropped dead, and he was carried out and buried. A short time passed and the wife, Sapphira showed up. Peter gave her the opportunity to come clean. She chose to stick to the story that she and her husband had agreed they would tell. The irony they selfishly, agreed on greed. In like manner, she also dropped dead. This teaches us the possible consequences of being greedy and or selfish.

Moreover, the example of Ananias and Sapphira gives us much to consider. Pointedly knowing the difference between what is truly ours and what belongs to God. How many times have we been greedy, stingy, and or selfish when dealing with God? How often have you asked God for His gifts, but you didn't want Him, the giver? How often have you known what was asked, and even required of you, but chose to do things your way? There are sins of commission and sins of omission. The things you omitted to do, were they just thoughtless, careless, and or forgetful; or were they deliberate greedy and or selfish acts? Was it tithes or offerings you didn't want to pay? Was it prayers or messages that you didn't want to say? Was it somewhere you did or didn't want to go? Was it a certain restraint or love and kindness you didn't want to show? Was it a reverence or a prayer, was it the good news we just didn't want to share. We do these things, sometimes thinking we are benefitting ourselves. But not always recognizing the adverse effect on others. More so how God looks at how we handled that situation.

Have you ever considered how much help is needed for what we call self-preservation? No man is an island, and at some point, and time we will see that we need the help of others. Their preservation is what will bring life to ours. For instance, when flying on an airplane, the instructions given by the flight attendants are clear. They state, if you are traveling with a small child and the emergency landing sign comes on, you are instructed to put the oxygen mask on yourself first. But the ultimate strategy is for everyone to survive, knowing that you have a better chance of helping the child live, as opposed to the other way around.

Let us consider the book of Genesis, the 37th – 46th chapter. A series of events amongst brethren and their differences and distain. Here we have a gifted, blessed child named Joseph, who was loved and favored by his father Jacob, but despised by ten of his eleven brothers. Their jealousy and selfishness, caused them to collectively conspire to kill him. However, the oldest Reuben convinced them to refrain from killing him, but to throw him into a pit. His intent was to return later, retrieve him, and bring him back to their father. The others unbeknownst to Reuben, sold him into slavery instead. This was done to spite their father. They had no concern how their father would feel knowing that the oldest son of his favorite wife was gone. Ironically as it was then so it remains to this day, someone is always trying to gain at the expense of others. Opportunists sell others into slavery for their self-gain. Slave masters oppress while relying on the strength, and ability of their slaves to sustain them. Imagine if that pharaoh had been so power struck, arrogant and spiteful enough to ignore Joseph. Of a certainty thousands of lives would have been lost.

There is an allegory of the long spoons, there's even videos. (https://youtu.be/IG_AELnZqEQ) This story is

Blessed With Less

attributed to Rabbi Haim of Romshishok, but has been repeated, edited, revised and paraphrased by many. This is said to depict the difference between heaven and hell. One major issue it addresses is selfishness. Here everyone is confined to one place, at the same time. Nowhere to run, nowhere to hide; no escape. Everyone is hungry, and they have plenty enough food, but their arms are too short to get the food to their mouths. Howbeit they are all provided long spoons. The spoons are too long, and their arms are too short to feed themselves. However, by putting their pride aside and acting unselfishly they can all survive if they would just feed each other. They can't be but so greedy, in as much as they are codependent. They also can't be spiteful to a point where they don't feed others, otherwise everyone starves because there is no one left to feed anyone. This depiction helped me coin a phrase that I use quite frequently simply put: "Everybody Eats, or Everybody Dies". I've used it interchangeably in various situations and scenarios; during sporting events and in business settings.

It's even more amazing how many of these philosophical stories are based on biblical principles. this Bible is full of examples showing us what we should and should not do. Time and time again we see the plight of the greedy and the selfish, but not many passages call spite by its' name. Anyone can be affected by these negative attributes. It doesn't matter your age, sex, class, profession or title. Even a prophet called by God; such was the case with Jonah, who was told by God to go and preach. He was sent to Nineveh an Assyrian city; in this modern day, we recognize that city as northern Iraq. Jonah a Hebrew, didn't like the Ninevites and initially refused to go on this assignment. Not because he was afraid, but because he was selfish and spiteful. His argument to God was that if he went and preached, they would repent. He knew if the people repented God would save them, and he didn't like them; so he didn't want them to be saved. As one of God's chosen people he was too selfish to share God with others in need. He spitefully preferred that they were judged and punished. Unfortunately, Jonah didn't consider the ramifications of his actions initially. He created a downward spiraling effect for himself. Our success is almost always tied to some form of interaction with others. Everyone has a job to do. If you are the preacher, preach, if you are the leader, then lead, if you are the follower, then follow. The response of others doesn't dictate your success, just do your job, without malice.

Moreover, anyone can be the target of these not so nice emotions. Even Jesus Christ became the subject of such. Jesus reaffirmed the writing of the prophets concerning the Son of man, to His disciples in Luke Chapter 18. In this dissertation, Jesus repeated the prophesies which stated, "He shall be delivered unto the Gentiles, and shall be mocked, and spitefully entreated". He clearly mentioned spite as the motive for how He would be dealt with. Not by strangers but by those who were supposed to know who He was. So as not to appear as the aggressors, they passed the buck to the Romans. Knowing their power hungry, carnal, egotistical, self-centered mentality. How cynical can one be to deliver someone to one whom you believe is an unjust judge? In this day and time that would be as manipulative as, bringing a blood or crip gang member to the Latin king gang for resolution, while telling them this rival faction claims he's a king.

Blessed With Less

In contrast, for those who might not be able to see themselves so easy, I offer this typical scenario. Have you ever been clothes shopping and saw "other people", pick up several garments, discard them and then repeat that process until the place was a wreck? Often, they are accompanied by a friend or family member, who might ask them, "are you just going to leave those clothes you pulled off the shelf or hanger all over the place?" To wit their common, priceless response is, usually one of the following:

a.) I don't work here.

b.) That's what "they" get paid for.

c.) They knew when they took this job they would be cleaning up behind folks.

d.) Please; which is generally proceeded by a pronoun associated with either the person they are addressing and or the mood they are in; re: girlfriend, girl, man, sister, brother, child, negro, or some other derogatory, and degrading title.

I am by no means suggesting we as patrons become a part of the janitorial services committee, but I ask with all due respect, which category(s) a person like that falls in? Are they just feeling entitled? Is it greed that caused them to pick up so many items? Was it selfishness that caused them to grab items to prevent others from getting them, as if there was no more in existence? Or was it spiteful, taking items they obviously didn't even want themselves?

Chapter 9 Greedy, Selfish, Spiteful

This mentality is so prevalent in our current day it's somewhat frightening. In most countries, communities, political arenas, religious institutions and even families. There are no exceptions, mankind in general continually does evil. Their greed and quest for power, money, position and prominence is clear and present. Greed will cause you to become paranoid. You will no longer trust anyone. Your only concern will be the preservation of more than you can handle. That will grow and expand to being selfish. Some of us won't even tell of the goodness of God. We believe if someone hears our testimony they will ask for some of our blessing. How selfish can one be, refusing to give glory to God ? That's outright spiteful behavior.

In the Gospel of Luke, the angel of the Lord appeared announcing the birth of the Christ child. "Suddenly there was with the angel a multitude of the heavenly host praising God, and saying, Glory to God in the highest, and on earth peace, good will toward men". Note it didn't say ill will toward men. The covetous want what belongs to others, the stingy refuse to share, and the spiteful do this with an ill intent. God commanded us to love our neighbor as our self. This leaves little to no room for selfishness, but on the contrary, selflessness is what should be practiced. His word admonishes us to feed the poor and help the needy. How can we carry this out if we are greedy? At the conclusion of the matter, less greed, less selfish and less spiteful, help us to be more like Christ. For sure more Christ-like, positions us to be blessed.

Chapter 10

Love,
Integrity,
Righteousness

"What is the definition of love? Can you give me a good description of love"? Can you tell me how and when you know it's love? Can you smell love, if so does it have a distinctive aroma? Is it visible to the naked eye or do you need a microscope or possibly a telescope to see it? Is there a definitive feeling or taste? Can you turn it on and off?

It's amazing how one word, with so few letters can be so complicated and powerful. Over the years I've heard many say that they "love but aren't in-love" with some other individual. This alludes to the notion that there are different types and levels of love. It's a shame we must now go through such extreme measures in qualifying what type of love we are talking about. Most will agree, the one they're looking and hoping for is "true love". Many can only give examples of mere aspects of love, but most cannot explain the very essence thereof. Probably because, God is love itself. In as much as He is too vast to be trivialized, compartmentalized, or reduced to one dimension, we do our best as mere mortals can, and give descriptions, based on our finite understanding. We give analogies, metaphors and clever clichés, all still only aspects of Him.

Chapter 10 Love, Integrity, Righteousness

Despite the inability to adequately explain it, we continue to give our opinions. There are one thousand, one hundred and eighty-seven (1187) songs with love in the title; Note, that's in just the secular realm alone. The longest known love poem according to the 2017 Guinness book of world records contains 291 stanzas and is 2,900 lines long. The poem published in 1846, is titled Marina. It was written by Andrej Sladkovi and describes an unfulfilled romance between the author and his muse. The previous record holder is Rajinder Tumber, it contains 2,413 words. Ironically, his poem, entitled "Divine Verse" wasn't addressed to any specific individual. He is a hopeless romantic that is still looking for love.

Those who can't sing or write poetry find other forms of expression, all in the name of love. Some the average person would say are subtle gestures, yet considered exciting, and appreciative, but normal; like sending flowers, candy and or a card. Then there are others that are a bit extreme, like getting a tattoo with a "loved ones" name or maybe even a picture. Giving well wishes or even a proposal on the big screen at a sporting event. People with disposable funds may rent a blimp or plane to sky write a greeting. Then there's the over the top, dare I say outlandish. Some were so big they made it into the Guinness book of world records. Some of the individual record holders include giving up sleep, food, and even going to the bathroom alone, for extended periods of monitored documented time. Moreover, there were some joint efforts that required equal participation: the longest hug was 24 hours and 33 minutes. The longest kiss 58 hours and 33 minutes. Most hugs given in a 24-hour period was 8,709. And last, the couple who, renewed their wedding vows 101 times, between the years of 1984 and 2017. That's an average of roughly 3 times per year. These are great expressions but does any of this show actual proof of true love?

Even the dictionary and encyclopedia have some difficulties providing one definitive answer. In fact, they give seven different variations of love. One is "Philia" the platonic, common brotherly love. "Storge" speaks of the love and genuine concern between a parent and child, or other relative. "Pragma" is that which is developed from longevity. This is often referred to as "standing in love"; which denotes an intentional concerted effort to stand firm on ones decision to be in love, as opposed to "falling in love". This suggests that by happenstance or coincidence, one without intent unwittily just fell in love. "Ludus" is an innocent flirtatious and teasing kind of love. Even though the objective is to become more acquainted through common methods, like dancing, laughter and other forms deemed clean fun. These are considered to be the purest types of love on the natural order, nothing lewd or illicit. "Philautia" was divided by the ancient Greeks into two types of love, playing both sides of the fence. I took notice of this subdivision of an already multi-ambiguous term. The first is a healthy love of self. Noting one must first love themselves in order to properly love others. The second is a selfish, narcissistic pleasure-seeking love. This is generally exhibited in very unhealthy ways. Then it shifts to "eros" which is the love of the body; a strong affection or adoration for another based on sexual desire. This one, most of us are acquainted with, it's the physical sexual embrace or copulation; which many refer to as "making love". This is where the term erotica came from.

Chapter 10 Love, Integrity, Righteousness

Based on the intense intricacy, I was curious as to how anyone could claim hold to making love; as if they were the creator. One should be careful not to confuse an obsession, infatuation or lust with love. Note: an obsession is an idea or thought that preoccupies or intrudes on a person's mind. Which allows you to become possessive but not necessarily with concern. Infatuation is: a short-term interest in something or someone, usually from a one-dimensional shallow perspective. These are all emotions with different intentions and levels of intensity. Lastly but most important and most needed is "Agape" love. This is the essence of the term love; the ultimate selfless kind of love. This is love for humanity. This love seeks the greater good in every situation. It doesn't operate on the "quid pro quo" philosophy, seeks nothing in return. It's charitable, compassionate, sympathetic and unconditional. This is the highest form of love. It is equated with the love of God for man.

The word "love" appears in the King James version of the bible three hundred, ten (310) times. One hundred, thirty-one (131) in the old testament and one hundred seventy-nine (179) in the new testament. In other versions of the bible, the word love appears over five hundred (500) times. There are also numerous references and inferences to the word, denoting the importance thereof. Ironically the word "love" is not written one time in a Qur'an. Some attempt to argue that the absence of the word love was due to the different culture and language. Can you imagine being with someone who never ever said, "I love you" verbally or in print? In one of my favorite movies "Ghost" Sam Wheat played by Patrick Swayze never would say he loved Molly Jensen who was played by Demi Moore. He would always say "ditto". No matter how many gestures or acts are performed, we all at some point and time want to hear it at least once. By the same token, we don't want to hear the words and then see actions which contradict those words.

God proves and extends His love daily. He also affirmed His love for us: "Yea, I have loved thee with an everlasting love: therefore, with loving kindness have I drawn thee" (Jerimiah 31:3). How much greater is it when given by God. "For God so loved the world, that He gave His only begotten Son, that whosoever believeth in him should not perish, but have everlasting life." (St. John 3:16). He continued saying "Greater love hath no man than this, that a man lay down his life for his friends" (John 15:13). After commending His love for us, He admonishes us to do the same, first toward Him; And thou shalt love the Lord thy God with all thine heart, and with all thy soul, and with all thy might" (Deuteronomy 6:5). Then on the same topic toward each other "This is my commandment, That ye love one another, as I have loved you" (St. John 15:12).

Unfortunately, opportunist take this ideology and twist it for their benefit. Can you count how many times and or scenarios where you heard someone use the phrase; "if you really love me you would..."? How many men have used that phrase to have their way with women ? How many women have used that phrase to manipulate men? All the children that were conceived by someone trying to prove their love. All the fights, wars and deaths caused by someone trying to prove their love. One bible reference stands out where this tactic was used. Delilah was paid to entice Samson, in order to find the source of his strength. "and she said unto him, how canst thou say, I love thee, when thine heart is not with me"?(Judges 16:15). Trying to prove his love, he divulged his heart and wound up bound and blind.

However, true love conquers all, it overrides emotions. Whether we are talking about how we should love, or how we should be loved. It enables us to be more patient, compassionate and forgiving. God's love extended far beyond man's actions; in that He provided a plan of salvation to redeem man back to Himself. Jesus is that plan; as a man He felt the pressure, and even prayed, "saying, Father, if thou be willing, remove this cup from me:" (Luke 22:42). He had a choice, to wit He chose to conclude in that same verse and sentence, with a very powerful declaration saying, "nevertheless not my will but thine, be done." In spite of this, many still continue to commit all types of acts under the guise of love. But we also have a choice. We can choose to keep pretending to love, performing acts in the presence of others, giving a false appearance of love.

Another ambiguous term people try to hide behind, is righteousness. Righteousness is defined as the quality of being morally right or justifiable. Conducting one's self under this premise can be very dangerous. Unfortunately, moral law is based on the majority vote and or the empowered party at that time. Depending on what country, state, city, or even neighborhood you are in, justifying yourself based on their rules could bring you into direct conflict with God. Almost everything is legal somewhere, but does it make it right? In some countries, a man can beat his wife to death in front of the authorities, and their law would concur that he was justified and acted righteously. In many states, the use of alcohol, tobacco products, and even some controlled substances are encouraged, legal and permissible. In some cities both prostitution and gambling are legal. Children can call the police on their parents if they believe their discipline was too harsh. In June of 2003 the supreme court of the United States reversed the decision on sodomy laws. Based on moral liberation of American sexuality, sodomy is no longer a felony crime. Without being an avid bible reader, most have heard the devastating story of Sodom and Gomorrah.

We are living in the last days, where men are calling right wrong, and also calling wrong right. Illicit, deviant behavior, and even prison recidivism is glorified. Yet prayer is not allowed publicly. The very mention of God is a potentially a punishable offence. According to a 2006 survey conducted by the "Pew Research Center" 69% agree that liberals have gone too far trying to keep religion out of the schools and government. And that 58% are in favor of teaching biblical creationism along with evolution in public schools, yet the opposition has been able to withstand these efforts thus far. We are living in a day and time where someone can break into your house and then sue you if they fall & get hurt, while they are there trespassing. Bottom line; just because it is legal, socially acceptable and or even morally justifiable, does not constitute you being righteous. This is more a state of apostasy as opposed to any form of righteousness.

If one is going to claim true righteousness, they must first qualify the standard with which they are basing their righteousness. I further contend, that standard must be the Word of God. We must ensure that we get all of His word, for mere aspects will give us only a portion of His intended message. Everything will fail except God's word. Jesus told His disciples, "except your righteousness shall exceed the righteousness of the scribes and Pharisees, ye shall in no case enter into the kingdom of heaven" (Matthew 5:20). Our manner of living must be circumspect as opposed to suspect. Our actions should be deliberate, and not measured by any other human being or their ideologies or philosophies or moral law. It's ironic that "moral law" is derived by what the people say is right for their culture. Through moral law, people have the "right" to choose how they want to be identified, they can legally determine their gender and sexual preference. One result of this liberal thinking is the forming of a controversial organization bearing the acronym: "NAMMLA" Which stands for "North American Man/Boy Love Association". Furthermore there's no law in the U.S.A. prohibiting a human from marrying an animal. There's at least seven countries where bestiality is legal, ironically in those same countries same sex marriage is illegal. And many individuals are exercising there "legal right" to do several things that was once shunned. Among the list is drinking alcohol, smoking marijuana, and casual sex.

Does legal make it right? The emphasized key root of the word in "righteousness", is "right". Our righteousness should have more depth than being politically correct, or merely carrying out a ritual or ceremony. Bear in mind, attending a religious institution for most is just a ritual. If you were to ask the average individual why they go to a church, mosque, synagogue, or a temple; you would receive several responses, most which would have little to do with the intended purpose of said institution.

Blessed With Less

True righteous living goes beyond our physical, psychological and emotional actions. It is a matter of the heart, and the intentions therein. Those intentions can be measured by our good character, probity, rectitude and uprightness. These characteristics can be found in one word; Integrity which is the quality of being honest, ethical, virtuous, truthful, trustworthy, and fair. Both righteousness and integrity are noted as possessing positive attributes, called qualities as opposed to having flaws. Integrity moves an individual to uphold a standard and conduct oneself in a consistent manner, especially when no one else is looking, or when you're sure you can get away with it.

In a legal aspect, intent is one of the hardest things to prove. Intent is specific, in that it involves the state of mind that an individual was in during the commission of a particular act; even if only temporary. Therefore, there are fewer trials charging individuals with premeditated, 1st degree or intentional murder, in spite of the fact they could prove who committed said murder. Many law suits are reduced in penalty, simply because of the lack of proof. In most relationships, committed parties first want proof of their partner's love, fidelity and at least a verbal declaration of intent. Others go through the extent of acquiring a prenuptial agreement. Businesses require disclosure forms, an investigation, along with contractual agreements, for their comfortability and protection. But when one is righteous that individual won't have any contention or dissension to any of those processes, but more importantly, they are not generally necessary. There is a bitter-sweetness, when dealing with intent. The true judge here, is God. One of the most famous sayings attributed to the late president Abraham Lincoln is about deception, which qualifies intent. That saying is "you can fool all the people some of the time and some of the people all the time, but you cannot fool all the people all the time". It seems need to say, but if you can't fool people, you certainly con not fool God. "God trieth the hearts and reins" (Psalm 7:9). "God judgeth the righteous, and God is angry with the wicked every day" (Psalm 7:11).

All things considered, there is a scripture that many may say is conflicting and somewhat disheartening. While the prophet Isaiah was observing the actions of people and their abundance of sin he said: "But we are all as an unclean thing, and all our righteousnesses are as filthy rags;" (Isaiah 64:6). Legalists and those looking for an excuse will say living righteously is impossible so why even try. And naysayers will contend this is a contradiction, noting that so many other scriptures encourage righteousness as a standard of living. Pointedly one verse definitively states; "He loveth righteousness and judgement: the earth is full of the goodness of the Lord'' (Psalm 33:5). How can this be, and how can we trust any of the words written in "this book". However, when one is attempting to live in true righteousness, they realize the only way in which they can comply with the acceptable standard, is to first learn the rules. It is incumbent on each individual to read, study and understand what is required. One is to know and understand, we can do none of these things with a fleshly mindset. The same way we inquire and investigate our companions likes and dislikes, we must do the same with God. Who takes a job without knowing what is initially required of them? We want to know the hours, the salary, the benefits and the duration. How many have truly asked God; what is required of "me"; without comparing or even inquiring about someone else? Or do we just presumptuously hope that this loving God will just do for us with no expectations? I will further ask, how many of us ask God to help us live beyond what our flesh and our minds can comprehend?

For a surety, God's word tells us "And ye shall seek me, and find me, when ye shall search for me with all your heart" (Jeremiah 29:13). He confirms that word out of the mouths of several witnesses. "Ask, and it shall be given you; seek and ye shall find; knock and it shall be opened unto you; - For every one that asketh receiveth; and he that seeketh findeth; and to him that knocketh it shall be opened" (Matthew 7:7-8). After all these examples and instructions, our integrity is what will cause us to act in the appropriate manner. God doesn't force us to serve Him. When you have true love, no one should be able to legitimately question your integrity. If you truly love God you will keep His commandments, that obedience is what makes you righteous in the sight of God. Once you've reached your limitations, He will then sanctify you with His righteousness. The scriptures on numerous occasions tell us to Love the Lord with all our hearts, might, minds and soul. You cannot love God more than He loves you. All three components have something very valuable in common; they cannot be bought. If you sincerely exhibit all of these attributes God has no other response than to bless you.

Do The Math

$$\frac{\text{LOVE} + \text{RIGHTEOUSNESS}}{}$$

$$= \text{INTEGRITY}$$

Chapter 11

Cursed,
Envious,
Poisoned

Ooh, you said a bad word; at least that's what I thought. As a child when I heard cursed I immediately associated it with profane language. I was totally oblivious to the notion that a person or a people could be cursed. Cursed by definition is: the expression of a wish that misfortune, evil, bad luck and or doom befall a person or group or even a thing. It is used to express annoyance or irritation. An individual may speak negatively, pronouncing ill will, ill fate or damnation of another. Using Sir Isaac Newton's third law of motion, which states: "For every action, there is an equal and opposite reaction". That being the general consensus and used more so in a physical realm, I noted the relativity and have surmised that cursed is the exact opposite of blessed. The lack of dominance should not be confused with a notion that the other entity does not exist.

Once I came to the knowledge that one could actually be cursed, I then enquired as how does one become cursed, and who has the power and or authority to pronounce a curse on someone else? Initially, my only reference to anyone, or anything being cursed was in fairy tales mostly during childhood. They all involved some incantation from a magician, witch or warlock. The list of stories we were exposed to was quite extensive. How well do you remember the following stories: Aladdin, Beauty and the beast, Cinderella, Enchanted, Hansel and Gretel, Little mermaid, Rapunzel, Shrek, Sleeping beauty, Snow white and the seven dwarfs, Stardust, The Girl with no hands, Wizard of Oz? Our minds were poisoned with all these myths, that had no real life, applicable value. The fact is there are real curses, and they have, can and will cause you to die, both naturally and spiritually. While researching curses, we found they actually started in the heavenly realm, when Lucifer showed his pride, jealous and envious character. Let us examine the five statements of condemnation Lucifer used attempting to usurp authority, in Isaiah 14:13-14, beginning with "I will":

1.
   a. "I will ascend into heaven"

   b. "I will exalt my throne above the stars of God"

   c. "I will sit upon the mount of the congregation in the sides of the North"

2. "I will ascend above the height of the clouds"

3. "I will make myself like the Most High"

Lucifer didn't just get puffed up, he began to hate the very authority who gave him his position along with anything and anyone that was favored by God. Unfortunately for us, God chose mere humans to love. Lucifer therefore became the enemy of mankind. He also wanted that which was already designated for Christ, (Ephesians 1:20-23).

We must take note of the difference between pride and envy. We also should further consider that although similar and somewhat synonymous, there is yet a very distinguishable difference between jealousy and envy. Pride causes one's ego to swell up in their own conceit. One with this form of pride, individuals presents, and even sometimes believes they are more than they actually are. Jealousy is a three-person situation, whereas envy is a two-person situation. Jealousy is a reaction to the threat of losing something (usually someone) to someone else. This means when you are feeling jealous you are often feeling envious as well." With jealousy, you at feel a sense of entitlement or even ownership. In general, you possess what you are jealous over. This is why, God Himself stated: "for I the Lord thy God am a jealous God" (Deuteronomy 5:9). He didn't want His people bowing to any other god. Envy on the other hand is a reaction to lacking something. A envious individual not wants what not only doesn't belong to them but more so, what belongs to someone else.

After countless examples, throughout every walk of life, one must wonder, why anyone would be envious. There is enough God for everyone to receive their fair share of attention. Knowing that there are very distinctive identities of every human, inquiring minds might want to know why. I contend if we spent half the time and effort in ourselves, as we use investigating everyone else, we wouldn't have time to be envious. We would discover that we all have a unique role and purpose. Even when we have certain qualities and abilities, that doesn't give us the right to infringe on someone else and their purpose. Everybody cannot be the boss, on the contrary, we are supposed to be one body of baptized believers, working toward one goal. The Apostle Paul while teaching on the true church which is, the body of Christ stated: "For the body is not one member, but many" (1st Corinthians 12:14). He compared the spiritual gifts to our natural physical bodies. One of the highlights was the applicable point that diversity was necessary, and that same diversity must be used in unity. Furthermore, all parts/gifts/people have a place, we should therefore strive to be the best we can be at being ourselves. If you perfect being the best you, and I, the best me, where would envy find room? Or as Paul said: "that there be no schism in the body" (1st Corinthians 12:25)

Nonetheless, Lucifer apparently influenced a third of the angels that he would be exalted, and they should join in this mutiny against God. This brought them all into a place that they didn't belong in, and were not capable of functioning in. As a result, lucifer and his imps, were not only cursed, but cast out of God's abode. He didn't leave peacefully, but fighting an obviously losing battle. He not only lost his position, but he also lost his name, and would now be known by the name Satan. One powerful tactic of war is to weaken the head by attacking the body. Since he couldn't outright beat the creator, he went after the creation. The earthly manifestation is clear in Genesis the 3rd chapter in the garden of Eden. Eve was deceived by Satan, Adam was encouraged and listened to bad counsel and they both fell from thee favor of God. The serpent was cursed because it was used to deceive man (Genesis 3:14). The woman was cursed, losing her equal place with man and destined to have pain doing what she was naturally made to do; in child bearing. The ground was cursed as the earthly punishment to man. And man was now subject to the nature of sin and penalty of death. Which is the same Adamic nature that all mankind since then was born with. In the beginning God created mankind in His image. But after the fall mankind was born in the image of Adam (Genesis 5:3).

Satan, wanting desperately what belonged to God, enviously convinced Adam and Eve, that they weren't who they were. That was the ultimate slap in the face to have the creation volunteer to go against God. What would it take for you to go against God? If someone offered you cyanide or arsenic, and you had a full understanding of the substance and its effect; would you voluntarily consume it? That might be a bit extreme and probably deemed suicidal. How about if a cook, waiter or waitress at an eating establishment, dropped your food on the floor, but attempted to serve it to you anyway; would you receive it? That would probably be considered nasty and might make you sick. Well everything was perfect and in order, but then Adam and Eve took the mental poison. It was subtly deceptive, but severely devastating.

Poison in biology is a substance that causes disturbances in organisms, usually by chemical reaction or other activity on the molecular scale, when an organism absorbs a sufficient quantity. Mental poison is having un-resourceful, negative thoughts constantly in your mind. Those negative thoughts include but are not limited to: Anger, hate, ill-wishes, envy, depression and doubt. Mental poisons are introduced through various methods; lies, black magic, hypnotism, or a simple suggestion. There's an old saying "if it looks like a duck, walks like a duck and quacks like a duck then it must be a duck". Can you imagine being able to convince that duck that he is not a duck? Seems absurd, but Satan convinced Eve that she wasn't like God. Even though the scripture Genesis 1:26-27 declared that in His(God's) image and likeness created He them". He further convinced her that God wasn't being forthright with them, saying "ye shall not surely die" (Genesis 3:4). Satan cannot create, he can only manipulate. He didn't have the authority to change the names of Adam and Eve, so h influenced them to believe they were something other than the image of and like of God. Without knowing who you are you also will question your own authority. If allowed to continue, you will question your very nature, causing you to veer into a deviant behavior, to the extreme of sexual immorality even unto bestiality. They had dominion over everything but forfeited that when they temporarily forgot who they were.

The same tactic has been used throughout history and is still effectively used to this day. Fact The scripture declares: "There is nothing from without a man that entering him can defile him; but the things which come out of him" (Mark 7:15). However, anything that stays in the body long enough can and will affect the body. A paper cut is small and virtually insignificant, unless that open cut is exposed to germs. That once minor cut now has the potential to become infected, which if not treated could cause gangrene which could lead to the loss of that finger, entire arm or even death. How much more subtlety can the mind be poisoned? The slightest thought planted in your mind could alter your perception. It is hard to qualify how much and how long it will affect an individual. If you were poisoned how and or when would you know? Medicine for one individual may be poison for another. Just as we don't all have the same chemical balance, neither do we have the same level of understanding, resistance or tolerance. This is why two individuals can consume the same type of alcohol, in the same amount, at the same time, yet have two totally different reactions. One may only feel calm or numb, but the other may be diagnosed as being alcohol poisoned. Just as there are variables that dictate the outcome of our physical bodies, so it is with our mental and spiritual selves.

Furthermore, there are several manners in which one can be poisoned. One of the most common methods is oral consumption. Young children are taught not to take candy or any other substance from strangers. On the acceptable occasion of trick or treating we were always warned about paying attention to who and where they obtained their treats. Noting the realistic possibility that someone might taint any food product that wasn't properly sealed. At least once a year we would watch the fairytale of "Snow White" and the seven dwarfs. In this story a wicked, extremely jealous queen, wanting Snow White dead, prepared a poisoned apple just for her. Any young person that has ever attended a party, was always reminded

Chapter 11 Cursed, Envious Poisoned

never to put your open drink down, to avoid the possibility of someone poisoning said drink. When I worked in the jail system, if we responded to an alarm while eating, any open food was to be discarded, fearing that someone might take advantage of the opportunity to put something in the unattended food/drink product.

However, there are yet other ways for poison to enter the body. The hardest is to inject a toxin directly into the blood stream. Very much like drugs that are introduced via "mainline" injection. For those who were somewhat passive they would use a technique known as "Skin popping" where the drugs would be rubbed on in an abrasive manner, noting that drugs can be absorbed through the skin. Lastly there are drug that enter through the nasal passage. On September 11th, 2001; many individuals had various reactions to fumes they breathed in. several have died, and many more are sick, even to this day. Some were in direct physical contact with substances at the ground zero sight, others were miles away, yet several were still affected. This reminds us that poison can enter through any orifice and can also seep through your skin. The only thing needed is to be exposed. That realty it true in the physical, emotional and spiritual aspects. The same way natural poison affects the physical body, so it is with our emotional self. What generally happens when someone tells you that your companion is unfaithful? Even when you don't want to believe it, something happens that now causes you to question their every movement. Sometime not so direct, but for sure you now pay more attention to anyone they talk to. You begin to monitor more closely when and where they go.

Blessed With Less

What are the effects of one being poisoned spiritually? You begin to question your spiritual leaders and ultimately God. "Satan himself is transformed into an angel of light" (2nd Corinthians 11:14). This scripture is somewhat of an oxymoron, although not a contradiction. The envy Satan has, causes him to try and copy, dare I say impersonate, everything that God is and has. When he approaches or influences us humans, he appears in a form that we would receive. As he did Eve, he attempts to deceive us every opportunity he gets, every day. Anything he can do to get us to doubt, fear, or become prideful, selfish, spiteful or envious; know that you have been poisoned. One of the oldest governing power strategies was deportation. This tactic deprived people of the strengthening power being of united, through isolation. If Satan can get you away from communication with God, it is easier to persuade you. Let's face it, is you child more, or less likely to be seduced by a predator if you are present. At the very least they would look to you for your approval. So it is when we refrain from assembling ourselves together. It is a bit of a paradox; by exhibiting these characteristics you become poisoned and when you are poisoned you exhibit these characteristics. They enhance one another and are easy to entertain. The questions become more frequently asked, and more intense. Questions I would be surprised if you haven't heard, or maybe even asked yourself. Questions like, is all of "this" really necessary? That "this" could be, paying tithes and or offerings; a holy standard, frequently attending a church; being subject to a spiritual leader. Do we really need to pray, everyday? Do we need the holy ghost? Is the holy ghost just a gift? Do I have to be baptized? If so how must

Chapter 11 Cursed, Envious Poisoned

I be baptized? If there is a God why does He let so many bad things happen in the world

One of the greatest tricks in existence doesn't involve any magic or wizardry. That trick is convincing humans that the devil isn't real. The notion is simply if there is no devil, and no hell, then maybe we don't need a God to protect us, or maybe there isn't a God at all. "The fool hath said in his heart, There is no God" (Psalm 14:1). The omission of information can be more damaging than misinformation. Ommissioon denotes a posture that say I either don't believe or I refuse to receive. Consider how many children convince their friends that "no one will find out" about the mischief they are about to engage in. You've heard the poisonous lines: "no one will know", "it's fool proof", "it won't hurt", "it's not like it will kill you", you can't get pregnant on your first time". Rikers Island is a jail complex located in Queens New York. It is completely surrounded by water. It is primarily a detention center yet there are consistently over ten thousand inmates housed there daily. Many of the residents are there simply because they thought they wouldn't get caught. Unbelievably sadder, is knowing that the majority are inherently planning on returning there after being released. They have been convinced this is a better lifestyle therefore don't look for anything productive to help prevent their return. While some are envious of the seemingly lavish lifestyles of a drug dealer and therefore attempt to emulate them; others are envious of those who have been in jail and entreat it like a badge of honor. A lot of the younger population were told by some older criminal they should take part in a crime spree because they were minors and the law had to be more lenient

Blessed With Less

on them. The poison of misinformation is still permeating the minds of people all across the globe.

I'm sure most have heard of cases of sibling rivalry. The younger will argue that they can never do what the older ones can do. In contrast, the oldest sibling complains that they have to be bothered by the younger. They will further argue that the parents are more liberal with the younger one, so much so they can do things the older never could get away with. These perspectives often evolve to jealousy and even envy. But the truth is the younger eventually get older, and are then able to do almost anything. However, the oldest has something the younger will never have. The oldest had the privilege to have the parents all to their self with no other children to share with. Unfortunately, this mindset is prevalent in the "church" world. Almost everyone is now claiming they are "children of God". As a direct result, when negative things happen, we hold to a position that we're being tested. Some even believe they are being disciplined, and will half quote the two following scriptures "as a man chasteneth his son, so the Lord thy God chasteneth thee" (Deuteronomy 8:5); and "For whom the Lord loveth He chasteneth" (Hebrews 12:6).

So yes, there is a God, all this and more is necessary. God chose the method of preaching to speak to the masses. Any society or organization that does not have order and leaders is subject to chaos.in answer to all the important questions and false posing statements, I reaffirm. the holy ghost is a gift, but it is necessary in conjunction with water baptism. That baptism is full submersion and should be performed in the name of Jesus. I refuse to believe that Peter who walked with Jesus and opened the first Christian church misunderstood what Jesus told him directly. After being filled with the holy ghost Peter preached this message: "Repent, and be baptized every one of you in the name of Jesus Christ for the remission of sins, and ye shall receive the gift of the Holy Ghost" (Acts 2:38). That was supported by the following: "Neither is there salvation in any other: for there is none other name under heaven given among me, whereby we must be saved" (Acts 4:12). Prayer is a necessity. Just as Adam talked to God every day, we should also, not just on some days but every day. Lastly, once Adam and Eve fell, sin entered the world. When sin entered it caused a natural disorder, we are therefore now subject to sickness, disease, calamity and death. But there is an antidote. "If my people which are called by my name, shall humble themselves, and pray, and seek my face, and turn from their wicked ways; then will I hear from heaven, and I will forgive their sin, and will heal their land" (2nd Chronicles 7:14).

Until we are transformed by the renewing of our minds, we must realize, the possibility of being cursed is a reality. Cursed is negative a pronouncing over your life and or the affairs therein. There is a general curse spoken by God over all mankind formed after the likeness of Adam, and then there are specific curses based on our current behavior. Take comfort in knowing, no man without express permission and authorization from God can curse anyone who is in alignment with God's word. The patriot Jacob answered Balaam in this manner: "how shall I curse, whom God hath not cursed? Or how shall I defy, whom the Lord hath not defied?" (Numbers 23:7) In other words, the only way you can be cursed is if you distance yourself from God. Throughout the scriptures God through delegated authority, allowed holy men to pronounce curses on those who were contrary to His word. Some were personal, and some were generational. Note, generational curses no longer hold the same weight as shown in the question which was asked by one of the prophets: "What mean ye, that ye use the proverb concerning the land of Israel, saying, "The fathers have eaten sour grape, and the children's teeth are set on edge"? As I live, saith the Lord God, ye shall not have occasion any more to use this proverb in Israel" (Ezekiel 18:2-3). Again When Amaziah was twenty-five years old and began to reign as king of Judah in Jerusalem, he killed all who was involved with the death of his father(King Joash). "But he slew not their children, but did as it is written in the law in the book of Moses, where the Lord commanded, saying, The fathers shall not die for the children, neither shall the children die for their fathers, but every man shall die for his own sin (2nd Chronicles 25:4). Everyone is now responsible for their own decision as to whether they serve God and be blessed or not. Some were not announced as a curse per say, but through prophetic utterance, devastation was frequently denouncing of certain acts or ideologies; know you are not safe. We teach in word, to stay away from natural poison, to not be envious and more frequent than actual that we are not cursed but blessed. However, our actions are toxic, hateful and anything but blessed.

BLESSED to be an individual favorably spoken of by God

ORDAINED for a specific task in a specific season

PERFECTION, fulfilling who you are to your destiny

Chapter 12

Blessed,
Ordained,
Perfection

God bless you; a common verbal expression, said by millions in response to a sneeze. Is there any credence to the old habitual phrase? It is truly amazing how many individuals profess to be blessed. It's even more amazing what most people refer to when defining or qualifying what blessed is. Then you have the flip side, where people use the term as a condescending way to dismiss another individual. I've gone through extensive study, and have resolved that blessed of God, is not any of the following: luck, chance, superstition, pride, doubt, frustration, fear, feelings, less, lack, mediocrity, greed, selfish, spiteful cursed, envious or poisoned. Although it contains facts, a mere fact is not what blessed is. That brings us back to the question of what it is to be blessed? Are there different types and or levels of Blessings? Who is qualified to issue a blessing? What position do you have to be in to receive a blessing?

For starters, to be blessed is to have some type of gift bestowed upon you. Blessings received can be either tangible and or intangible; natural or spiritual; verbal and non-verbal. It can be inherited, genetic or imparted unto you. I also believe it's fair to say, and most would agree, there are both, blessings of God and blessings of men. Note you can receive a blessing without being blessed. For an isolated incident, action or possession does not in itself constitute being blessed. Unfortunately, sometimes the wonderful gifts given by men, were bombs in disguise. Thus, you can have a blessing which now becomes a curse and vice versa, a curse can turn into a blessing; but you cannot be blessed and cursed simultaneously. The scriptures declare, "ye thought evil against me, but God meant it unto good" (Genesis 50:20). That statement was made by Jacob's son Joseph, as he revealed himself to his brothers.

Many have looked at the struggle or plight, that our predecessors had endured, and have questioned whether they would have been able to see it through. Could you ever have pictured a slave becoming a hero, or called blessed? Quite honestly if you looked at the entire beginning of the life of Joseph, would you be able to identify him as one of the blessed by God? Let us begin, with a mini biography of just Joseph. His mother Rachel died giving birth to his younger brother Benjamin. He was raised in part by Leah, his father's other wife, who might I add was aware that Jacob Loved Rachel and not her. Leah had sons who despised Joseph for both his natural, and spiritual position, gift and blessing. These blood brothers, threw Joseph in a pit and left him to die. He was found by travelers who sold him into slavery. While in slavery he was falsely accused and thrown into prison, because of his integrity. Can you see what might have appeared as a curse or punishment? However, that helped propel Joseph into his destiny. God orchestrated the events that followed. Joseph was so blessed that God used enemy (slave traders) to pull him out of a hole. Even while in prison, Joseph remained consistent.

Blessed With Less

He exercised his gift, and continued to help others. He ultimately wound up in Pharaoh's house and second in command to all Egypt. Pharaoh gave him an Egyptian name "Zaphenath-paneah" which meant (God speaks)..He was given Asenath, the daughter of the priest to be his wife. With his royal position, he was given a ring, gold necklace and fine clothes. That blessing of position and power gave him the opportunity to exercise his blessed gift of wisdom and management which prevented the starvation all of Egypt, and many other affected areas, including his family who was living in Canaan during this seven-year famine.

Based on that previously noted, historical reference, I believe it is fair to say many people don't truly understand how blessed they are. We get so caught up with the appearance and misinterpreted notion of being blessed, we don't take the time to search it out from God's perspective. I heard the profound words of Spoken Word Artist Talaam Acey saying that: "God Himself could hang a halo over the head of some people and they would still refuse to believe they were blessed". In poetic form, he further stated:

"If you gave the average black man
Fifty thousand dollars on consignment
He'd cop a Rolex watch, get robbed for it
and spend the rest of his life wondering where the time went".

Those that can muster up enough insight, are still generally limited. Many will boast of being blessed with their mother's looks, genetically; wit of intelligence, intuitively, their father's work ethic, constructive ability, or even their insurance or property, inherently. But can any of those compare to being blessed with the spirit of God? How many are aware and truly grateful that they have the fruit of the spirit? How many can recognize, acknowledge, accept and carry out their call; while saying they're blessed with it?

Many that do recognize a call, but see only the struggle, and not the blessing initially. Even Job, although called perfect by God, cursed the day he was born. Somehow, someway, he couldn't see how blessed he was. He was singled out, by name, and volunteered by God, to represent, challenging Satan. God was sure what he placed in him. Could God brag on you like that? Can he count on you? God blessed Job with love, joy, peace, patience, kindness, goodness, faithfulness, gentleness, self-control, along with long suffering, and noted integrity. He never went off on his accusing friends, or his contrary impatient wife. He didn't complain, or lose his mind over the material wealth he lost. Rather he first worshipped the Lord then his verbal reply was: "Naked came I out of my mother's womb, and naked shall I return thither; blessed be the name of the Lord" (Job 1:21). Even at the news that all of his children died, the scripture declares: "In all this Job sinned not, nor charged God foolishly" (Job 1:22).

Very much like Job many of us are called and ordained to an assignment. Ordained is derived from the root word order. It is to invest, appoint, confer, install and or grant authority for an individual to operate in an official capacity or manner. For those who are apprehensive about or have abstentions to taking orders remember, "The steps of a good man are ordered by the Lord: and he delighteth in his way" (Psalm 37:23). Most ordinations are performed by men but orchestrated by God. This process is especially used for ministers and priest, but as seen with Job no title is necessary. God calls us into our future. Some jobs are prestigious, and others are trying to say the least. On the extreme examples was Jesus Christ; "He is despised and rejected of men; a man of sorrows, and acquainted with grief" (Isaiah 53:3). Lo I come (in the volume of the book it is written of me,) to do thy will, oh God" (Hebrews 10:7).

In spite of what it may look like know that God has a specific plan for you. And if God says anything to you or about you, just know that he has already equipped you for the task. God does not call the qualified, rather He qualifies the called. Vs_26-"For ye see your calling, brethren, how not many wise men after the flesh, not many mighty, not many noble, are called:" vs_27-"But God hath Chosen the foolish things of the world to confound the wise; and God hath chosen the weak things of the world to confound those things which are mighty;" vs_28-"And the base things of the world, and the things which are despised, hath God chosen, yea, and the things that are not, to bring to nought things that are;" vs_29-"That no flesh should glory in His presence" (1st Corinthians 1:26-29). God is not concerned with what you think you have or can do. He wants to see how much He can do through you. God is not impressed by stuff, but is moved by what you do with what you have. To that cause, God in His infinite wisdom, gives us what we need to work with. "For as the rain cometh down, and the snow from heaven, and returneth not thither, but watereth the earth, and maketh it bring forth and bud, that it may give seed to the sower, and bread to the eater:" (Isaiah 55:10). The system is in place, He gives to you, so you may give, and as you give He gives you more to give. Thus, if you really want to be blessed, give all. I am totally convinced that your gift is not for you. If you have the gift of healing, is it so you can be well? If you have the give of song, is it so you can sing to yourself? If you have the gift of knowledge or wisdom, is it so you can sit in your own conceit, having counsel with yourself? You may not be a minister in the sense that you speak from a pulpit, but we are all called to minister which means to serve. It could be something as simple as a person genetically blessed with height retrieving an item from a top shelf for some that cannot reach it. Or as extreme as carrying n incapacitated person from a burning building. "for unto whomsoever much is given, of him shall be much required (Luke 12:48). We serve God by serving people. You cannot give more to God or to His people in His name than He will give to you. By the same token You cannot expect to withdraw more than you deposit. If you want perpetual blessings you must continue to be a blessing.

When you do a really good job of serving in any capacity, others tend to qualify your performance. They will grade or rate your performance with an adverbial phrase, such as: good job, great job, excellent, fabulous, magnificent or even perfect. I find many people refraining from the later, some because they don't know how to explain perfection in a human being. But most because they don't believe anyone can be perfect.

However, if you will indulge me in my folly there are several scriptural references I would like to present for consideration. "Noah was a just man and perfect" (Genesis

Blessed With Less

6:9). "the Lord appeared to Abram, and said unto him, I am the Almighty God; walk before me, and be thou perfect" (Genesis 17:1). If it were not possible, why would God tell him to do it? I contend, anything God tells us to do, God also equipped us with the ability to do it. In contrast "when Solomon was old, that his wives turned away his heart after other gods: and his heart was not perfect with the Lord his God, as was the heart of David his father" (1st Kings 11:4). Clearly a difference is noted between king Solomon and his father king David. It certainly could not be their actions, but that difference was identified distinctively and specifically as their heart. So as not to give the illusion that this mindset and heart condition is isolated to the royal family, let us remember "Asa's heart was perfect with the Lord all his days" (1st Kings 15:14). "Then the people rejoiced, for that they offered willingly, because with perfect heart they offered willingly to the Lord: and David the King also rejoiced with great joy" (1st Chronicles 29:9). "There was a man in the land of Uz, whose name was Job, and that man was perfect and upright, and one who feared God, and eschewed evil" (Job 1:1) and finally, "for the eyes of the Lord run to and fro throughout the whole earth, to shew Himself strong in the behalf of them whose heart is perfect toward him" (2nd Chronicles 19:9).

Perfection does not mean you may never make a mistake. Perfection is the mindset and posture which you regularly maintain. It's operating with pure honest intent. Let me be clear in adding, you must ensure that, the pureness we express, is in line with God's commands, laws, and will. For there are soldiers who carry out their orders with diligence and integrity, but they are fighting for the wrong cause. The previously mentioned examples of those who were noted as perfect, were doing so without the holy ghost, which is now available to all men to obtain. So there clearly is a manner and aspect of perfection attainable to all.

Furthermore, there is another level of perfection, that goes beyond our normal physical ability. Jesus while teaching on the mount of Beatitudes, said: "Be ye perfect, even as your Father which is in heaven is perfect" (Matthew 5:48). Paul picked it up and said: "Having therefore these promises, dearly beloved, let us cleanse ourselves from all filthiness, of the flesh and spirit, perfecting holiness in the fear of God" (2nd Corinthians 7:1). This is a great part of the miraculous redemptive process of God. "And the very God of peace sanctify you wholly; and I pray God your whole spirit and soul and body be preserved blameless unto the coming of our Lord Jesus Christ" (1st Thessalonians 5:23). "For by one offering He hath perfected for ever them that are sanctified" (Hebrews 10:14). Once we reach our limitations, our extremities become God's opportunities. He then does the miraculous by putting the super on our natural. It is of a certainty, the shedding of blood on Calvary which redeems mankind. "Now unto Him that is able to keep you from falling, and to present you faultless before the presence of His glory with exceeding joy" (Jude 1:24). His blood covers us the same way the blood covered the children of Israel in Egypt. The same God back then is the same today, yesterday and for ever more. It's His mercy that takes those who were undeserving and presents them clean and blameless. As much havoc, rebellion and dissention that was among the children of Israel, yet through an act of obedience, God saw fit to provide a way for them to escape the death angel. Nothing logical about the ritual that was performed, but by faith, and faith is not logical.

How does one qualify to be numbered among the blessed? Our 1st task is to glorify God, while doing so we are to seek out what our job is, and finally to do that job while continuing to glorify God. Although we may praise with our physical bodies, the level of worship and glorifying of God must be done in the spirit, which takes faith. "But without faith, it is impossible to please Him" (Hebrews 10:23). If you are not pleasing God, why would He bless you? If you are subscribing to and or relying on any of the following: Luck, Chance, or Superstition; your Power or Authority, how does that fit into God's plan for you. If you are operating in any of the following: Envy, Greed, Spiteful, poisoned, doubtful, mediocrity, Pride and Frustration, your feelings or fear; again, I will pose the somewhat rhetorical question, how can you be blessed? Possessing only one of the good qualities or defeating only one of the bad flaws, is a start but not enough.

Don't be fooled by appearances, especially based on the natural eye. Whether it's a favorable opinion or an unfavorable one, just make sure it's a Godly one. For you may be looking at Joseph, Job, or even Lazarus. On the flip side you may be looking at King Saul, Pharaoh or a rich man. "But the Lord said unto Samuel, Look not on his countenance, or on the height of his stature; because I have refused him: for the Lord seeth not as man seeth; for man looketh on the outward appearance, but the Lord looketh on the heart" (1st Samuel 16:7). It's amazing how much the scriptures qualify when giving instructions. "Brethren, if a man be overtaken in a fault, ye which are spiritual, restore such an one in the spirit of meekness; considering thyself, lest thou also be tempted" (Galatians 6:1). In each situation, God expresses the need to look beyond the deed and or the person and to look at their heart. The catch is, in order to do that you have to be spiritual. Sometimes it's just hard to see the forest for the trees. Sometimes it's where you are or where you are looking. The success of an individual is greatly affected by their environment. When you are blessed, nothing can stop you from flourishing, however, you may require more assistance and attention. Lot planted himself in an unproductive place but because of his connection to Abraham who was blessed, God sent him a personal escort out of that wicked city before destroying it. Joseph on the other hand was planted by God, with the intent to use him to save many.

Even when you have a gift, and are blessed, there are still variables that affect your blessing. Joseph was born with a gift, he was already blessed, but someone with authority still had to bestow authority on him for him to use his ability. We as humans don't make people, however we do empower, and sanction their ability to operate. When I was newly saved I asked God to keep me in a position to be a blessing. Hind sight is twenty twenty; for I didn't understand the full level of responsibility associated with that request. I was under the misunderstanding that in order to be a blessing, I must have more than enough to sustain myself, plus have a surplus.

Obviously, my perception and comprehension were obscure. I have experienced what God said through the prophets, which is: "for my thought are not your thoughts" (Isaiah 5:8). But as we read further down to the tenth verse we find it stating: "for as the rain cometh down, and the snow from heaven, and returneth not thither, but watereth the earth, and maketh it to bring forth bud, that it may give seed to the sower, and bread to the eater". There is both a natural and spiritual perspective presented here. We have nothing on our own, our gifts, talents and abilities all come from God. He gives us these thing to sow, which is to disburse. Spiritually that seed is the word of God, which we don't create, but we issue or plant that which God gives us. So, we now clearly see that all we have to, do is be in a position to be used. Now I know, you don't need to have anything tangible to be a blessing. I have been instrumental in putting people in houses when I didn't have one myself. I put people through school, and they have more education than me. I've even put people on jobs making more money than I was making. The more you give, the more God will give you to give. And other can eat what you share. A personal abundance is not necessary to own or even have. However, if you are in the correct posture and position, in God's Timing according to His Qualification and you also have Love, integrity; you consistently praise you both have faith and work righteously and you are content with your lot, then you are perfect in that which you know, and you are therefore Blessed.

You finally believe some others can be blessed, but somehow you personally can be blessed; especially with less. Noah: Preached one message for one hundred-twenty years and had on seven followers; his seed replenished the previously destroyed earth (Genesis 8). There were ten

Chapter 12 Blessed, Ordained, Perfection

plagues in Egypt, as noted in Exodus chapters 7-12; surely those that were not affected by those plagues were Blessed. "And five of you shall chase an hundred, and an hundred of you shall put ten thousand to flight" (Leviticus 26:8). Joshua & Caleb, was sent out by Moses to spy the land of Canaan along with ten others. They all came reporting similar finding but with a different perspective. Incidentally they were the only one from their generation spared after coming through the wilderness (Numbers 13). Gideon after reducing his army from thirty-two thousand down to only three hundred men defeated the Midianites and Amorites (Judges 7). A widow woman of Zarephath was commanded to sustain the prophet Elijah, during a famine and drought. She had a little oil and a handful of meal. She had already resolved you was going to have her last cake and die. God blessed her to feed the prophet Elijah, her son and herself many days. The prophet Elijah having nowhere to go was first sustained by a raven then by this widow (1st Kings 17). On another occasion, Elijah, without any other human, had face off with four hundred and fifty prophets of Baal on Mount Carmel (1st Kings 18). In this order Job lost his oxen, his asses, his sheep, his camels, his servants and his entire family. His three friends tried to convince him to confess to being out of order, his wife told him to curse God and die; but he held on to his integrity and continued to bless God.

Daniel was alone many days, the most memorable was in the lion's den, or as I heard it so cleverly presented, "the lion's in Daniels den". God showed everyone who was truly blessed. Jesus blessed over five thousand, feeding them with just two fish and five loaves of bread (Matthew

Blessed With Less

14:19). There were twelve baskets of scraps left over, to wit, he fed another four thousand the next day (Matthew 15:34-35. There was a poor widow woman who gave an offering as did others, but Jesus took note and stated that she had given more than them all (Luke 21:1-4). There was a man who was lame from birth. The man was brought daily to the temple gate called beautiful, wherein he would beg for money. A multitude passed him every day, but on this day two men Peter and John we're going to prayer. When they beheld him begging Peter said " silver and gold have I none, but such as I have give I thee: In the name of Jesus Christ of Nazareth rise up and walk" (Acts 3:1-6. There were only two of them they had no money, no gold, nothing tangible; but they were able to bless a man. The man was lame, had no income, but was in the position to be blessed. The appropriate response was walking, leaping and praising God. Peter, James and John we're taken by Jesus to a high point on the Mount of transfiguration. There appeared unto them, Moses And Elias. Peter was in awe and said, let us build three tabernacles one for each of them. While he was speaking a voice out of a bright cloud said: "This is my beloved Son, in whom I am well pleased; hear ye Him" (Matthew 17:5). They fell to their faces in fear, but Jesus came and touched them telling them to arise, and be not afraid. "When they had lifted up their eyes, they saw no man save Jesus only" (Matthew 17:8). That not only alludes to, but reveals and confirms that only one Tabernacle is needed, and Jesus represents all three. There's an old Greek joke that says: "Christians are so poor; they only have one God". While some try to make gods out of almost any and or everything, I am here to remind you there is only "One Lord, One Faith, One Baptism, One God and father of all, who is above all, and through all, and in you all." (Ephesians 4:5-6). John the revelator was banished, excommunicated, and isolated on the island of Patmos. He had less companionship, less communication and less friends. But he also had less distractions and less negative influences. However he had a long time with God and was blessed to see and write the book of Revelation, which is the Revelation of Jesus Christ. The words he shared blessed every believer in Christ with some understanding but more importantly, with more hope for our eternal future.

All those witnesses were given as examples. Most of them questioned, wavered and even doubted; repeatedly asking God to prove Himself. On one particular occasion noted in the 6th chapter of Judges, a prophet came to the children of Israel telling them as a collective group not to fear the gods of the Amorites. Following that an Angel of the Lord appeared personally to a judge named Gideon, calling him a mighty man of valour, while assuring him that the Lord was with him. Gideon 's first response was the common question: "if the Lord be with us, why then has all this befallen us?" this specific question came about because they were being oppressed by the Midianites. Gideon then asked for a sign to prove that it was God talking to him. The Angel instructed Gideon to place both meat and unleavened cake on a rock, then he caused fire to come out of that rock and consume it. Gideon was convinced the Lord was speaking and he was excited. Not many days after he again asked God to prove Himself, specific task which he chose; to wit God honored his request. The very next day Gideon asked for a third sign with specificity; again God answered. Why do we as a people continue to ask God to prove who he is? If He did it before, He can do it again. If He did it for them then, He can and will do it for us now. Stop worrying about what you think you can't do.

Most humans with any sense, feels a level of inadequacy when challenged by anyone; much more so when challenged by God. Some feel they are not prepared enough, smart enough, strong enough, good enough; simply undeserving. I've heard countless individuals say: "as soon as they get straight they are coming to church and they're going to serve God". Unfortunately, most never make it, mostly because they are relying on their own intellect, power, intelligence and resources. I don't know how much I can stress we are never ready if we are operating in self. However when we decide we are going to listen to the instructions given and carry them out trusting God; at that point He we'll show Himself mighty and remind you and anyone watching you, who he chose to bless.

Furthermore, there are over one hundred (100) examples of characters in the Bible mentioned without ever divulging their name. It's important for us to know God's work is more important than our name. If we seek the one who blesses more than the blessing we will have both. Our desire should be that His will be done more than our name being mentioned.

"Finally my brethren, be strong in the Lord, and in the power of his might" (Ephesians 6: 10). "I beseech you therefore brethren, by the mercies of God, that you present your bodies a living sacrifice, holy, acceptable unto God, which is your reasonable service" (Romans 12:1)

Chapter 12 Blessed, Ordained, Perfection

all the preceding examples started with nothing tangible, yet both tangible and intangible results were produced through them. Jesus declared, "where two or three are gathered together in my name, where am I in the midst of them" (Matthew 18:20). Where there is unity, there is strength. Blessed individuals work with their hands find work. Blessed individuals study to show themselves approved. But if you really want to be blessed, give.

Moreover, you don't have to be horticulturist to understand that the harvest is always greater than the seed. You don't plant an oak tree in order to grow another oak tree; you only need an acorn which is the seed of that tree. There is no need to waste an entire orange to produce more oranges; you only need an orange seed. One of the smallest seeds in the world is the mustard seed. That tiny seed grows to become one of the greatest of all herbs. It's not a house plant, but becomes a tree reaching heights between six (6) and twenty (20) feet; as referenced by Jesus in Matthew 13:31-32). However, Anything God blesses that does not reciprocate, is deemed non-productive. There was an occasion when Jesus while in Bethany was hungry. He saw a fig tree seemingly in full bloom, for it had leaves on it's branches, however, it had no fruit. Because it was not producing what God created and ordained it to produce, Jesus cursed that tree. (Matthew 21:17-20). The disciples marveled at how fast the tree withered, for it withered away in a day.

God has an endless supply of both natural and spiritual blessings, and He rains on the just as well as the unjust. He only gives in abundance to those who are not only available but also willing to give all. Ultimately we must all come to the realization That this realm that we live in is temporary. Eventually we must all give all. The good part is that we have a say on how and when we give our life. "To live is Christ, and to die is gain" (Philippians 1:21). After you have given your time and your substance you must qualify what and or who you gave it to. When we give our all we reduce our acclaim While Simultaneously promoting Christ. We have proved through our faith and works how less attention to ourselves is the greater gain. The more you give for Christs' sake, The less you have in this carnal world and the more blessed you are. Just think of all the patriots and our ancestors that sang the following song lyrics: "My Soul looks back and wonders how I got over". Innovatively learning how to survive on the beggarly elements, feeding families with leftovers or even scraps. I'm reminded of the prophet Daniel refusing the King's meat and choosing to eat pulse (vegetable soup). Ironically those that stood their ground and followed Daniel looked better in appearance than those who chose to eat the so called high end meal.

Remember only God can create something from nothing. If it appears that you have nothing or seemingly less than most and you are still not only surviving but productive; know for a surety, you are indeed **BLESSED WITH LESS**.

The End

The ≠ Poet Joel

Chapter 14 Afterword – About The Author

About Joel B. Parker, the Author:
By Chaplain Thomas G. Peters

Although his work appears in many anthologies in many countries, this is only the second published work containing solely the work of Joel B. Parker. It is also his first not written in poetry. I have been listening to and hearing his poetry for many years. When I questioned him about this specific book and in particular, its non-poetic format, Joel readily admitted that this was not anywhere in his portfolio or even in his imagination; however, while being considered to speak before an affluent crowd he asked, "what am I going to say to these people who considered themselves to be better than most"? He states that he received a clear definitive mind-blowing answer through the Holy Spirit which simply said: "Tell them you're Blessed with Less". He further stated that the spirit was so heavy on him that he wrote the first chapter on the train from Brooklyn to Manhattan which is only a forty-minute ride.

This is: **The End**
of this book,
however it is
NOT the end of this journey.

Follow us on Instagram: **@ThePoetJoel**

Email: **ParkersPoetryPlus@gmail.com**
www.ParkersPoetryPlus

View Parker's Press Release
https://brandfeatured.com/api/uploads/7654277-links.pdf

Let me add many other works can be witnessed and personally experienced in person at:
Morning Star Highway Church of Christ
869 Halsey Street {corner of Saratoga Ave}
Brooklyn, NY 11233

This is a church where all are welcome. you can come as you are but it's hard to stay as you are. Come be a part of this Life Changing experience

ADDITIONAL BOOKS:

Poetically Correct *From* Ground To Glory

"Poetically Correct Short Stories"
Shushan's Shenanigans (The Book of Esther)
Nebuchadnezzar's Nightmares (Daniel Chapters 2 & 4)

The Weak STRONG Man (The Life of Samson)
The Defiant Giant (1st Samuel)
To Nineveh or Not (Jonah, Chapters 1-4)
The In-Love In-Laws (The Book of Ruth)
Signs of The Judgement (Beginning of The End)

(*You Are The*) "HELP IN CRISIS"

PARKERS POETIC PUZZLES – VOL. I

http://www.ParkersPoetryPlus.com
Email: ThePoetJoel@gmail.com
IG: PoeticWitnessWear

OTHER ITEMS / WORKS AVAILIBLE:

POETIC WITNESS WEAR
{Imprinted Garments}
Combination of: Silk Screen,
Embroidered & Cad-Cut
T-Shirts, Sweat-Shirts
Caps, Hats
Custom Jackets: wool/Leather, Nylon, Denim}
Laser Engraving

http://www.PoeticWitnessWear.com
http://www.ParkersPoetryPlus.com

Creator/Inventor of the
   "HOLY GHOST MIRROR"
http://www.HolyGhostMirror.com
Email: HolyGhostMirror.com

I.C.E.D.
Illuminated Custom Etched Display
Call :   (716) JBP-ICED
Email: JBP.ICED@gmail.com
http://www.IcedByThePoet.com